Teach Yourself to Sail

B J Doty

Teach Yourself to Sail

Get out on the water. Be safe. Have fun.

Copyright © 2012 B. J. Doty

TABLE OF CONTENTS

TABLE OF FIGURES

INTRODUCTION

If you're interested in learning to sail, you might be considering getting some professional instruction, either taking a group class or getting one-on-one training. My advice: don't. There are a few fatal flaws I've found, which all the classes I've encountered seem to have in common.

First, they're expensive. There really is no secret, super-complicated science behind sailing that's worth hundreds of dollars and weeks of your time. The knowledge you need is simple and practical. That is to say, you need practice more than you need instruction. Spend your time and money on getting a boat and getting on the water. Don't sit in a classroom or read a bunch of books (Yes, I'm aware that you're reading a book right now, but this one specifically designed to be as short as possible).

The second problem with classes is that they're just too comprehensive. What does that mean? Well, sailing requires a bit of knowledge about a lot of different subjects – physics, nautical rules, knot tying, motorboat maneuvers to name just a few. Classes tend to get into way too much depth on each subject, when all really need is a basic understanding. You don't need to know how to navigate using a nautical chart and a compass if you have a GPS. You don't need to know a hundred types of knots, just a few that you'll actually use aboard a boat.

The third problem, I'll just call the establishment. Forgive me for sounding like a hippie, but sailing is supposed to be fun. You don't need a former marine yelling at you because you forgot to loosen the boom vang. You also don't need to be taken through a defined, rigorous pathway in your quest to become a sailor. Most classes will start you off with tiny boats and slowly progress up to larger ones. There's no need you can't start out on a midsize (20 – 40 ft) yacht as long as you're careful and understand the dangers.

HOW TO USE THIS BOOK

This book is designed specifically for those interested in **daysailing**. The primary goal is to get you sailing on decent sized **cruiser**, preferably one that's large enough to have an inboard motor, as fast as possible. There are only three basic rules I want you to follow while reading this book and learning how to sail.

RULE #1. DON'T HURT YOURSELF.

Priority number one is always safety. If you use reasonable caution and respect the natural forces that you are attempting to harness while out on the water, you will have no problems. But the fact is, there are many bad things that can happen to you or your crew if you aren't careful: drowning, hypothermia, hypothermia plus drowning, getting concussed by the boom, getting concussed by the boom and then subsequently drowning… you get the idea. Be bold, be adventurous, but don't be reckless. The vast majority of boating accidents are the result of poor or reckless decisions, and are entirely avoidable.

RULE #2. DON'T HURT THE EQUIPMENT.

If you've decided to learn how to sail, you already know this, but sailing equipment is expensive, especially the boats! If you own your boat you don't want to damage your prized investment (not that boats are a great investment to begin with). If you're chartering or borrowing someone else's boat, you would like to be able to charter or borrow from them again. And no matter whose boat you're on, you never want to bump another boat and have its owner coming after you for repair money. For the most part, it's not too difficult to avoid running into other boats on the open water (although I've come pretty close). The tricky part is in the marina, getting in and out of the dock, avoiding buoys, and the Chinese fire drill that happens in busy marinas at the start and end of the day. Remember what you learn here and you'll be fine.

RULE #3. HAVE FUN. CAPTAIN'S ORDERS!

That's it. Follow rules #1 and #2, and you really shouldn't worry about anything else. Have fun! That's the point, isn't it? It may seem obvious, but I want to make having fun a rule, because too many times, people get uptight about sailing. They become so focused on doing everything "right," learning all the fancy terminology, or displaying their maneuvering prowess for other boats, that they forget to have fun. OK, this is a confession, when I say "people," I'm talking about myself. I'll let you in on a secret: nobody cares. And everyone else is drunk. Be safe, and don't worry about anything else.

SAILBOAT BASICS

If you have even the slightest experience with boating, you know that there is a whole new language associated with it. Most sailing courses start off by making you memorize a list of vocabulary words. Sounds fun, right!

Fortunately memorization of the complete language of sailing isn't necessary. Yes, knowing the terminology is helpful, but most terms are useful primarily as a means of describing ideas when learning or discussing sailing. For example, it might be useful to know what a luff is when I'm describing to you how wind acts on a sail, or which telltales mean what, but in all my years sailing, I can't remember once using the word on board a boat – mainly because I'm often the only person aboard who knows how to sail. A rare few terms are actually used while sailing, but again, they won't help much if your crew doesn't know what you're talking about.

Regardless, I'm not going to start off by dumping a bunch of vocabulary on you. The approach I'll use is to define sailing terms as they come up. Also, if there's a key word that you don't know, check the glossary in the back and the odds are it'll be there.

That said, there is some basic orientation stuff that needs to be covered upfront, including the parts of a sailboat, sails, rigging, and directions. Feel free to give these sections a quick overview and only flip back if you need a refresher.

PARTS OF A SAILBOAT

Figure 1 illustrates the basic setup of a sailboat. The **hull** of the boat, consisting of the **cockpit**, the **cabin**, and the **foredeck**, is the main structural component of a sailboat. The front of the hull is called the **bow** while the back is called the **stern**. The side of the boat is called the **beam**, and top edge of the hull around the sides is called the **gunwale**.

The boat is steered using the **rudder** at the back of the boat which knifes through the water. The rudder can be controlled by a **tiller**, as shown, or a wheel that is mounted in the cockpit. The **centerboard**, an adjustable fin-like structure protruding underneath the hull, adds lateral stability to the boat. In larger boats, the centerboard is replaced by a **keel**, a heavily weighted fin that is permanently fixed to the hull.

The main pole that holds up the sails is the **mast**, and the **boom** supports the bottom of the **mainsail**.

Sail edges are described in terms of their **luff**, **leach**, **foot**, and **head**. The luff is the windward (front) edge of the sail and the leech is the leeward (back) edge. The foot is the bottom edge, and the head is the top point. The **tack** and **clew** of the sail are the windward and leeward corners for the sail, respectively.

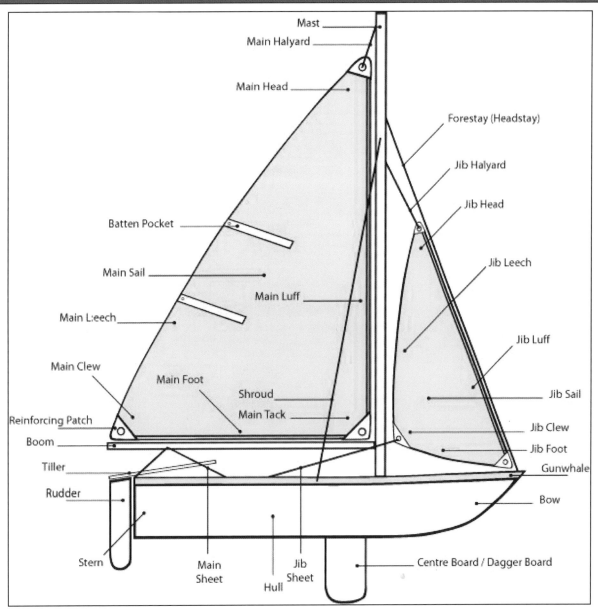

Figure 1: Parts of a Sailboat

SAILS

There are two basic types of sails on most sailboats, a mainsail and the **foresail**. The mainsail is mounted behind the mast and is supported by the boom. As the name suggests, it's the primary sail. Some smaller boats may only have a mainsail.

The foresail is used to add sail area and increase the wind power captured by the boat. Also, a boat that is designed for a foresail will be easier to steer if it is flying a foresail.

Typically, a sailboat has only one mainsail, but several different types of foresail can be substituted for one another. A foresail can be a **jib**, **genoa**, or **spinnaker**. Jibs come in different sizes, the smallest being a **storm jib**, and a genoa is basically just a very large version of a jib. For this reason, the terms foresail and jib are commonly used interchangeably. A spinnaker is a very large foresail used only under certain conditions and requiring a completely separate set of rigging from the jib.

Some modern sailboats have **furling** sails. A furling system on the jib allows it to be rolled up around the luff for easy storage. Otherwise, when not in use, the jib has to be completely taken down. Less common are furling mainsails which coil up inside a special hollowed out mast.

RIGGING

Rigging – or the ropes and cables that hold up and control the sails – is divided into two categories. **Standing rigging** is basically anything used to hold up the mast. This includes all types of **stays**, **shrouds**, and **spreaders**.

Running rigging, on the other hand, controls the sails. These include **sheets**, **halyards**, the **clew outhaul**, **topping lift**, **cunningham**, **boom vang**, etc. Sheets are ropes or **lines** that control the **trim** – or shape and orientation - of the sails. Halyards are lines used to raise the sails. The clew outhaul is a line that pulls the mainsail clew out to the end of the boom. The topping lift and downhaul control the height of the boom (or spinnaker pole). On downwind tacks, the jib clew can be held out using a **whisker pole**, which attaches to the mast.

A system of **cleats**, **blocks**, and **winches** is used to feed the lines around obstacles on the boat into a position where they can be easily operated. Cleats are used to hold a line in place. Blocks are essentially pulleys that change the direction of a

line. Winches are circular ratcheting devices that can be used to crank a line in if it's difficult to pull by hand.

DIRECTIONS

On a sailboat, directions are defined relative to the two important reference points: the boat and the wind.

Figure 2 shows the terms that are used to describe directions with respect to the boat. Naturally, **forward** or **ahead** describe the direction pointing to the front of the boat, off the bow. The opposite direction, behind the boat, is called **aft** or **astern**. The directions to the side of the boat are **abeam**.

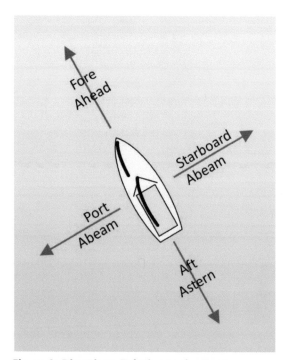

Figure 2: Directions Relative to the Boat

While looking forward, the right side of the boat is the **starboard** side and the left side is the **port** side. Remember, these directions are always relative to the boat. So if you're facing forward, the starboard side is to your right, but if you're facing aft, the port side is to your right. The major benefit of defining directions with respect to the boat is that they don't change based on which way you're looking.

Forward and aft tend to describe locations within the boat or parts of the boat, such as the forward deck, while ahead and astern tend to describe movements, e.g., full speed ahead.

Aside from the boat, a sailor must also know the wind. Figure 3 shows the common ways to describe a location or direction relative to the wind. The direction into the wind is known alternately as **upwind**, **windward**, or **aweather**, while that pointing away from the wind is called **downwind**, **leeward**, or **alee**.

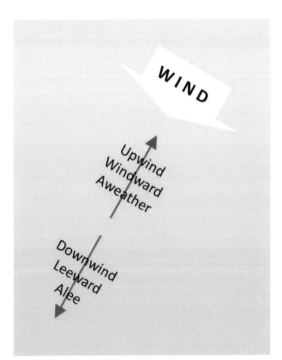

Figure 3: Directions Relative to the Wind

It is also important to be able to describe changes in direction aboard a sailboat, which are shown in Figure 4. Turning into the wind is called **heading**

up or **luffing up**, while turning away from the wind is known as **bearing away** or **falling off**.

Since the angle with respect to the wind changes during a turn, the angle and shape of the sails must be changed accordingly (we'll discuss this in more detail later). When the boat heads up into the wind, the crew must **sheet in** or **harden up** the sails, bringing the sails closer to the centerline of the boat. When the boat bears away from the wind, the crew must **ease off** or **loosen up** sails, letting the wind push them further away from the centerline.

The reasons why these changes in sail characteristics are necessary will become clear later during the discussion of how a sailboat works. For now, the terms are simply given as reference.

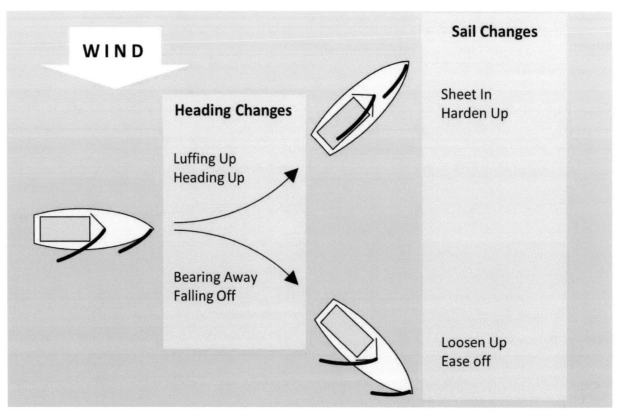

Figure 4: Changes in Direction

HOW A SAILBOAT WORKS

In this section, we'll discuss how wind interacts with a sailboat to propel it through the water.

First, it's important to note that by wind, we actually mean **apparent wind**, which is the wind "felt" by a moving object. More formally, it is the vector sum of the **true wind** and the velocity of the object (in this case a boat) as shown in Figure 5.

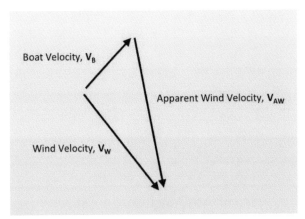

Figure 5: Apparent Wind Direction

Even with no wind, a plane can fly by creating apparent wind with its motion. If you play golf on a calm day, aerodynamic forces are still created on the ball by the relative motion between the air and the ball as it travels through the sky. These are two example cases where apparent wind is much more important that true wind due to the large speeds of the objects travelling through the air. In sailing, the boat's velocity is not that large, but it does effect the direction an strength of the apparent wind.

Throughout this book, the terms "wind" and "apparent wind" are used interchangeably. Unless it is specified that we are referring to the "true wind" it can be assumed that we mean apparent wind.

LIFT AND DRAG

Any time wind passes over an object – be it an airplane, a sailboat, a golf ball, a baseball, a rock, or even a person – the wind exerts aerodynamic forces on that object. Without delving too deeply into the physics of fluid dynamics, the forces created by wind passing over an object are due to acceleration of the wind air mass.

Essentially, when moving air molecules bump into or pass over an object in their path, they change direction or speed in some way. This change in direction or speed – called acceleration – of the air mass creates a force. You may be familiar with Newton's 2nd law of motion, simply stated as force equals mass times acceleration.

Some objects, such as parachutes, tend to primarily slow down or decelerate the wind air mass, while others, such as an airplane wing tend to deflect the air, changing its direction. Sails can act like parachutes or airplane wings, depending on their configuration.

The aerodynamic reaction force is most easily thought of as the sum of two components. Lift is the component of force that acts perpendicular or normal to the direction of the wind. Drag is the force component that acts parallel to the wind. Using the previous examples, airplane wing forces are dominated by lift, while parachutes create mostly drag.

In the context of sailing, the size of the total wind force on a sail and the relative contributions of lift and drag are dependent on:

1. The apparent wind
2. The angle of attack of the sail
3. The size and shape of the sail

The sailor determines the apparent wind felt by the boat (or at least its direction) by steering the boat.

The sailor can also control the sail angle of attack, the shape of the sail, and even the size of the sail that is exposed to the wind (limited by the full physical size of the sail).

SAIL ANGLE OF ATTACK

The **angle of attack** is simply a physics term that describes the angle between the **chord** of the sail and the apparent wind direction. A smaller angle of attack means the sail is aligned more parallel to the wind, while a sail with a large angle of attack is at more perpendicular to the wind.

Figure 6 illustrates how lift and drag contribute to the total wind force for different sailing directions. Notice that for a small angle of attack (the leftmost illustration), the total wind force is dominated by lift, while for a large angle of attack (right illustration), drag dominates. Also notice that when the boat is aligned nearly perpendicular to the wind (middle illustration), the sail angle – and the relative distribution of lift and drag – is nearly identical to that of the boat sailing more into the wind.

These concepts are fundamental to sailing. When sailing in the region from a direction pointing into the wind down to a point about perpendicular to the wind, the sail acts primarily as a lift generator, much like an airplane wing or airfoil. When sailing away from the wind, the sail harnesses drag forces, much like a parachute. In fact a spinnaker – which only functions on downwind tacks – is often referred to as "the chute."

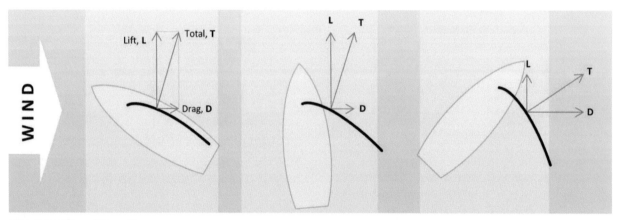

Figure 6: Lift and Drag Forces

SAIL AREA

Obviously, the size of a sail also affects the total aerodynamic force, but fortunately, the effect is fairly simple and intuitive. All else being equal, larger sail produces more force than a smaller sail.

The size of the sail area exposed to the wind can be controlled by either of the following:

1. Changing the actual sail, i.e., replacing the jib with a smaller jib or a genoa

2. Reducing the amount of the sail that is exposed to the wind, achieved by either **reefing** the mainsail or furling the headsail

SAIL SHAPE

The shape of the sail also effects the airflow around a sail and thereby the efficiency with which the sail captures wind forces. By shape, we mean the curvature of the sail in terms of:

1. The depth or **draft** of the sail
2. The **twist** of the sail

The aerodynamic effects of draft and twist very complicated, and the most efficient settings cannot be broadly defined. The simplest way to determine the best sail shape is to use feel or telltales – as we'll discuss later. In general however, there are a couple rules of thumb that can be used:

- Twist is best kept to a minimum.
- A flatter sail is better in stronger winds and while close hauled.

The shape of a sail is controlled primarily by the *angle* at which the sheet pulls on the sail. This angle is determined by the traveler for the mainsail and by the position of the fairlead for the foresail. Improperly set halyards, clew outhaul, topping lift or Cunningham can also lead to excessive draft or twist of the sail, but these are not typically changed while under sail to control sail shape.

MULTIPLE SAILS

So far, our discussion has only considered a single sail, but most cruisers have two sails, a mainsail and a foresail. The addition of the second sail complicates the airflow somewhat, but the basic theory for understanding wind forces are the same.

Practically speaking, when setting the sails, the only thing that needs to be kept in mind is that the foresail should not block wind from the mainsail. Interference from the foresail can occur if it is pulled too close to the mainsail on a close hauled tack. This can be corrected by loosening the foresail sheet slightly.

FORWARD AND SIDE FORCES

Lift and drag are useful for understanding the mechanisms of how wind forces are created, but to understand their effects on a boat, it helps to consider wind forces differently. Total wind force can also be separated into the component acting in line with the boat's heading and that acting perpendicular.

The **driving force** is the component of total wind force that acts parallel to the boat's forward motion, while the **side force** acts normal to the boat's forward motion, as shown in Figure 7. Notice that the total force for each sailing direction is the same between Figure 6 and Figure 7, the only difference being the orientation into which the total force is decomposed.

When sailing into the wind, only a small portion of the total force is harnessed as driving force. On the heading that is near perpendicular to the wind, although the total wind force is about the same, a much larger portion of it acts as along the boat heading. On the downwind **tack**, almost all of the wind force is captured as driving force and the side force is nearly negligible.

When the sail is operating primarily in lift, for the upwind and perpendicular headings, the total force is largest, but it is most efficiently captured on the perpendicular heading. On the downwind heading, the total wind force is even more efficiently captured as driving force. However, since the sail is now acting primarily in drag, the total force is smaller.

These two factors – the magnitude of the total force and its alignment with the boat heading – combine to affect the driving force. As it turns out, the heading with the largest driving force is the one that is nearly perpendicular to the wind.

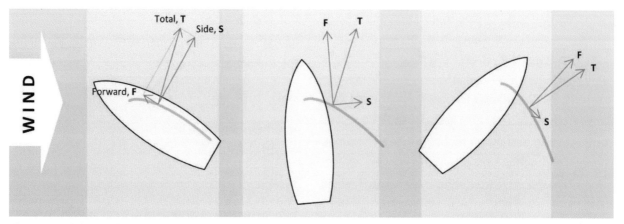

Figure 7: Driving and Side Forces

STABILITY

The driving force component of the total wind force is the desirable quantity that propels the boat, but the side force is parasitical, causing the boat to heel. Figure 8 illustrates this effect by viewing the side forces previously discussed in the vertical plane along the boat's beam.

As the boat travels through the water, the keel (or centerboard and rudder) generates lift and drag forces just like the sail. The side component of the total keel force reacts the side sail force equal in magnitude and opposite and direction (otherwise the boat would move sideways). These two forces act to rotate the boat (clockwise in this particular illustration) and are known as **heeling forces**.

Heeling forces are offset by **righting forces** – acting to rotate the boat in the opposite direction – including the hull buoyancy, the crew weight, and the keel weight.

As the boat heels, the size and location of buoyancy force changes. Buoyancy is proportional to the volume of water displaced by the hull and acts at the center of this volume. As the boats orientation changes, so does this volume of displaced water, which can be seen in Figure 8 as the portion of the hull that is beneath the waterline. Notice how it changes with the heeling of the boat.

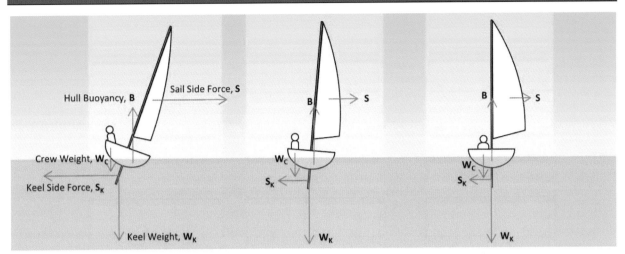

Figure 8: Heeling and Righting Forces

Heeling also causes the location of the keel weight (with respect to the center of rotation of the boat) to change. When the boat is flat, the keel weight acts in line with the rotation point and does not produce a moment. As the boat heels, the keel weight begins to produce a righting moment that becomes larger as the heeling angle increases.

The crew weight – or in reality the weight of any moveable object aboard the boat – can be adjusted to change its distance relative to the rotation point and thereby effect the size of the righting moment. More generally, the weight of the crew or other onboard objects is called **ballast**. To prevent or limit heeling, ballast is moved to the windward side of the boat, a.k.a. **topside**.

For each sailing direction and distribution of heeling and righting forces there is some heeling angle where an equilibrium is reached and the boat stops rotating. If not, the boat continues heel over until it is knocked down or capsized.

Figure 8 shows the equilibrium for each of the three heading discussed in previous sections. As

the side force becomes smaller, the heeling angle becomes smaller until a heading downwind where the side force is so small that the entire heeling moment can be canceled by only a small ballast or a minimal displacement of the keel weight.

Notice that by far the greatest righting force comes from keel weight. Imagine what would happen if the keel weight were removed. In that case – which is the configuration of most small dinghies and racing boats – the righting moment now depends primarily on the location of the crew. In order to offset the heeling moment, the crew must increase its distance from the rotation point, often beyond the boundary of boat. This process – which you might have seen in pictures of small racing boats where the crew hangs off the side of the boat using straps and ropes – is known as **hiking out**. As you can imagine, even the smallest changes in the location of the crew have a large effect on the balance of forces, the boat is much less stable, and capsizing is a common occurrence.

While heeling is arguably the most exhilarating aspect of sailing, it can be dangerous in high winds, and contrary to common belief, it reduces boat speed, all else being equal. Heeling changes the shape of the hull that is underwater, usually increasing the drag and thereby slowing the boat down. However, unless the boat has a very large base, such as a **catamaran** or **trimaran**, heeling is inevitable and the resulting speed reduction should not be given much thought.

POINTS OF SAIL

As we've seen, a sailboat harnesses wind forces differently depending on the direction it travels with respect to the wind. This direction is formally known as the **point of sail** or tack. Each point of sail has an optimal sail configuration that harnesses lift and drag forces most efficiently to propel the boat forward. We've alluded to these earlier, but the complete array of points of sail, and their formal names are shown in Figure 9.

Notice that there is an area directly into the wind that the boat cannot travel, known as the **no go zone**. If a sail points too closely to the wind, the air will tend to flow equally on either side of the sail and it will lose its airfoil shape and begin to flap loosely in the wind, much like a flag. In this condition, the sail is **luffing**, and does not capture significant aerodynamic wind forces. The boat cannot generate forward motion and the rudder loses its ability to steer. The boat is **in irons**.

The closest point to the wind that a boat can travel with full sails is called **close hauled** or **beating**. Typically the angle is about 45° to the wind. However it is sometimes possible to sail even closer to the wind depending on the wind strength, the hull and sail design, and the skill of the crew.

The point of sail directly downwind is known as a **run** or **wing-and-wing** since the sails are often set out to either side of the boat like wings of a bird.

Between beating and running is called **reaching** with the point nearly perpendicular to the boat called a **beam reach**. The area between a close hauled tack and a beam reach is called a **close reach**, and between a beam reach and a run is called a **broad reach**.

Notice also in Figure 9 that the different tacks are characterized as either starboard tacks or port tacks. This distinction, starboard or port, is determined by the *side of the boat over which the wind passes*. When the wind is coming over the starboard side of the boat, it is said to be sailing on a starboard tack, and vice versa.

General guidelines for the **sheeting angle** – the angle between the boom and the centerline of

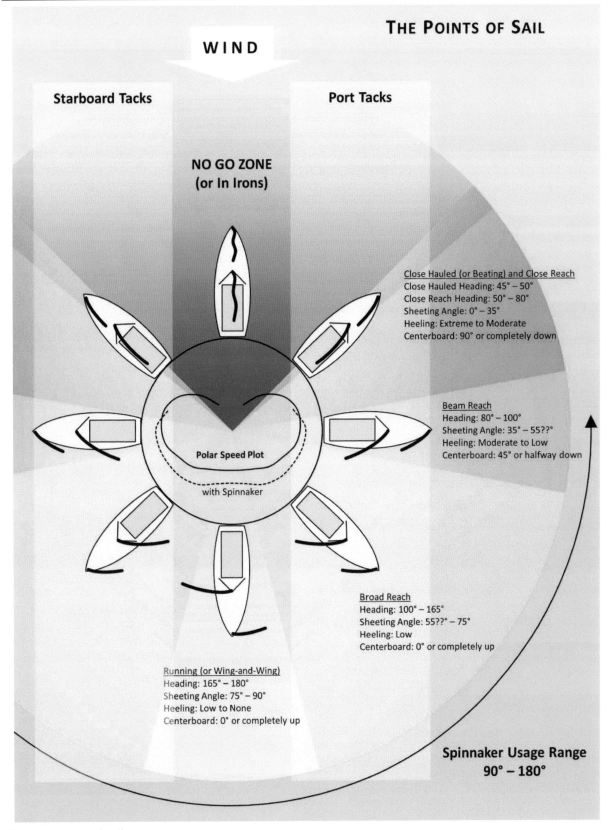

THE POINTS OF SAIL

WIND

Starboard Tacks

Port Tacks

NO GO ZONE
(or In Irons)

Close Hauled (or Beating) and Close Reach
Close Hauled Heading: 45° – 50°
Close Reach Heading: 50° – 80°
Sheeting Angle: 0° – 35°
Heeling: Extreme to Moderate
Centerboard: 90° or completely down

Beam Reach
Heading: 80° – 100°
Sheeting Angle: 35° – 55??°
Heeling: Moderate to Low
Centerboard: 45° or halfway down

Polar Speed Plot

with Spinnaker

Broad Reach
Heading: 100° – 165°
Sheeting Angle: 55??° – 75°
Heeling: Low
Centerboard: 0° or completely up

Running (or Wing-and-Wing)
Heading: 165° – 180°
Sheeting Angle: 75° – 90°
Heeling: Low to None
Centerboard: 0° or completely up

Spinnaker Usage Range
90° – 180°

Figure 9: Points of Sail

the boat – and centerboard depth are also given in Figure 9 for each point of sail. The most efficient sheeting angle depends on the size and shape of the sail, the strength of the wind, and other factors, but these guidelines are given as reference and to provide a starting point for each tack. For dinghies without a keel, the centerboard depth can be set to control side motion of the boat. It is not too critical, but in general, the centerboard is lowered as the boat sails closer to the wind.

In the center of the points of sail diagram is a typical radial speed plot which shows the relative boat speed for each point of sail. The solid line indicates the speed for a typical sail configuration using a jib as the foresail, while the dotted line gives the speed while using a spinnaker. As we've mentioned, the maximum driving force occurs on a beam reach, and it can be seen from the speed plot that this tack is the fastest point of sail. The spinnaker increases the achievable speed across the board, but is only operable on downwind tacks, as illustrated by the speed plot and the label showing the spinnaker usage range of 90° – 180°.

WIND

STANDARD COASTAL WINDS

Essentially, wind is caused by pressure differences between two volumes of air. The high-pressure air rushes into the volume of the low-pressure air to equalize this imbalance. Absent of storms, pressure fronts, and other weather patterns, these pressure imbalances are caused by temperature gradients.

Most relevant to the sailor are the wind patterns created over bodies of water by the temperature differences between air over the land and air over the water. Since water stores heat much better than land – or rock, dirt, etc – its temperature responds more slowly to changes in sunlight. Incidentally, this phenomenon is responsible for areas near the ocean usually having more "temperate" climates than areas farther inland at the same latitude.

Consequently, during the day the air over land is warmer than the air over water, causing the air to rush towards the land, creating an onshore wind, as shown in Figure 10. Conversely, at night the land cools faster than the water and the reverse effect occurs. The air over land is cooler than the air over water, causing an offshore breeze as shown in Figure 11.

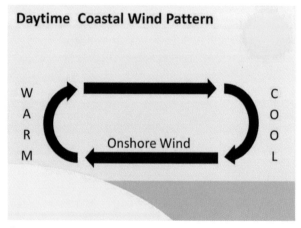

Figure 10: Daytime Coastal Wind Pattern

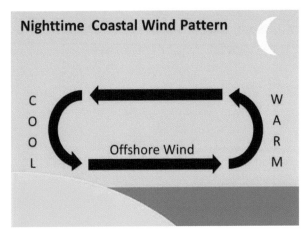

Figure 11: Nighttime Coastal Wind Pattern

WIND STRENGTH

Prior to heading out on the water, it is important to understand the strength of the wind that you'll be dealing with. If the wind is too strong, it's better to simply avoid going out on the water than deal with the difficulties and dangers of high winds, particularly when you are a beginner.

Wind forecasts are widely available, and those relating to sailing can usually be found under the label, "marine forecast." The National Weather Service publishes marine forecasts on the internet (http://www.nws.noaa.gov/om/marine/home.htm) that include information on water waves and swells along with wind speed.

When forecasts aren't available, it is useful to have a method for judging wind speeds based on visual indicators. The Beaufort Wind Scale, shown in Figure 13 was developed in the early 1800's by a British naval officer for just that purpose. The scale relates wind strength descriptions to visual indicators, and the actual wind speed in knots. It is not meant to be memorized, but is a useful tool for evaluating wind speed forecasts given in knots or estimating wind speed from visual indicators.

I've also added the common wind warnings: Small Craft Advisory, Gale Warning, Storm Warning, and Hurricane Warning. The best way to use this scale, or any wind forecast, is to help determine when NOT to sail. Anytime the wind speed approaches that of a Small Craft Advisory, it is best to stay ashore, particularly if you're a beginner.

WIND WARNING FLAGS AND LIGHTS

The wind warnings added to the Beaufort Wind Scale can be found in marine forecasts and reports, or they can be communicated using flags or lights as shown in Figure 12.

Again, any time you see or hear of a wind warning, it's best to stay ashore.

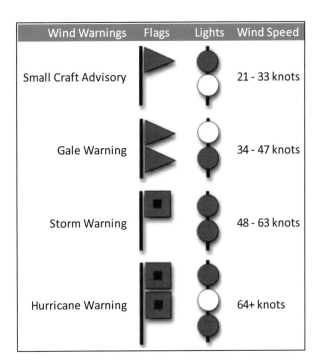

Figure 12: Wind Warning Flags and Lights

Scale	Windspeed (Knots)	WMO Classification	Indicators	Sailing Guidelines
0	< 1	Calm	Smooth, flat, mirror-like sea. Smoke rises vertically and leaves are still on land.	Small dinghys can barely make way under sail. Larger cruisers require motor power.
1	1 - 3	Light Air	Slight sea ripples, crests with no foam. Smoke drifts, wind vanes are still.	Dinghys make steady progress. Cruisers still need motor.
2	4 - 6	Light Breeze	Small wavelets without breaking. Wind felt on face, wind vanes stir, leaves rustle.	Dinghys reach good speed with full sails. Light cruisers may way under sail.
3	7 - 10	Gentle Breeze	Crests begin to break, scattered whitecaps. Light flags are entended, small twigs move.	Ideal dinghy conditions. Cruisers make steady progress
4	11 - 16	Moderate Breeze	Wavelenghths increase to 1-4 ft, frequent whitecaps. Dust is lifted, small branches move.	Too much wind for inexperienced dinghy sailors. Most cruisers reach hullspeed, some need to reduce sail area.
5	17 - 21	Fresh Breeze	Wavelengths at 4-8 ft, abundant whitecaps, some spray. Small trees sway and tops of larger trees move.	Inexperienced dinghy sailors will be capsized. Ideal cruiser conditions, but some must reduce sail area.
6	22 - 27	Strong Breeze	8-13 ft wavelenths, crests are foamy with spray. Large tree branches move, whistling in telephone lines.	Small Craft Advisory. Dinghys and cruisers should stay ashore.
7	28 - 33	Near Gale	Waves 13-19 ft high, foam streaks downwind off breakers. Large trees sway, resistance felt if walking against the wind.	Small Craft Advisory. Cruisers at sea should head for shore or prepare to ride out the storm.
8	34 - 40	Gale	Large 18-25 ft high waves, streaky foamy crests abundant. Twigs break off tress, walking is difficult.	Gale Warning. Only minimum sail area exposed to keep steerage control.
9	41 - 47	Strong Gale	High 23-32 ft breaking waves, foam and spray may reduce visibility. Slight structural damage to roofs, chimneys, and fences.	Gale Warning. Sails should be down. Tiller thrashing is only means of control.
10	48 - 55	Storm	Very high 29-41 ft waves, dense blown foam, lowered visibility. Significant structural damage, uprooted trees.	Storm Warning. Cruisers may be capsized or pitchpoled.
11	56 - 63	Violent Storm	Extremely high 37-52 ft waves, driving foam, very low visibility. Severe structural damage.	Storm Warning. Extreme danger, boats should stay away from shore, capsize or knockdowns possible.
12	64+	Hurricane	Huge 45ft+ waves, sea completely white, near zero visibilty. Catastrophic structural damage.	Hurricane Warning. Sailors at sea will be fortunate to survive.

Figure 13: Beaufort Wind Scale

Hull Speed

As a boat's hull passes through the water, it creates waves emanating from both the bow and the stern. In the water behind the boat, the waves cause a wake. On the boat itself, the waves are felt as drag resistance, tending to slow the boat down.

The distance between wave crests, or wavelength, of both the bow and stern waves is dependent on speed. As the boat travels faster, the wavelength becomes larger. At some speed, when the wavelength is equal to the length of the boat, the bow waves and stern waves add together to dramatically amplify the drag resistance felt by the boat. The speed at which this occurs is known as the hull speed of the boat, which is given by the following formula:

$$s_H = 1.34\sqrt{L_H}$$

Here, L_H is the length in feet of the hull at the waterline, and s_H gives the hull speed in knots.

While it is certainly possible for a boat to sail faster than this speed, it takes much more force to overcome the drag resistance and increase speed. So hull speed is a useful estimate of the peak speed under normal sailing conditions and without the spinnaker.

Knots

Modern cruisers typically have instrumentation that tells you the boat speed in a nice easy digital readout. However, it is also possible to measure the speed in a more primitive way. By tossing something – preferably biodegradable – into the water at the bow and measuring the amount of time it takes for the object to pass the stern, you can calculate the speed of the boat.

Speed is simply the distance traveled (the length of the boat) divided by time. Of course it's important to convert the quantities into the desired units.

In fact, the origin of the term **knots** being used as a unit for nautical speed is rooted in this crude method of measurement. Sailors used to throw a rope into the water and based on how many knots in the rope passed through their hands in a given time period, they could determine the boat speed.

History aside, a knot is simply a **nautical mile** per hour. Formally, a nautical mile is equal to one minute of latitude, which converts to about 1.15 miles. The usefulness of the knot unit becomes obvious if you ever try to navigate using a nautical chart, which is laid out on a grid of latitude and longitude lines. For a given speed in knots and time in hours, no conversions are necessary to map a distance traveled onto a nautical chart.

SAILING TACTICS

We've seen how a sailboat works. Now we'll discuss the more practical matter of controlling a boat. Since this book is primarily directed toward cruisers, for now we'll assume that you're operating a keelboat. Later we'll cover some things that are specific to dinghies and some motoring tactics to get you out to sea.

RAISING AND LOWERING THE SAILS

On a cruiser, the sails are typically down at the dock and they stay down until the boat is at sea. Of course, if you have no motor, the sails must be used to cast off, but we'll discuss that later. For now, we'll assume that the boat is out at sea with the sails tied down.

RAISING THE MAIN

The mainsail is raised first, and this can be done with the motor idling. The boat should be pointed with the bow facing into the wind. This alignment means the sail will be luffing when raised, making it easier to bring in the halyard and less likely that the sail will fill unexpectedly and knock the boat around.

The boom vang should be loose so that it does not resist the tension you'll put on the main halyard. The mainsheet should also be somewhat loose for the same reason, but it shouldn't be completely free since you don't want the boom swinging around in an uncontrolled manner.

When the boat is pointing into the wind and the boom vang and mainsheet are loose, the cover and ties can be removed from the main and the halyard brought in to raise the mainsail. The halyard should be able to be pulled in most of the way by hand – if not, there may be something

resisting it, such as the boom vang, or it may be caught – and then brought the final one or two feet by using a winch.

Once the sail is fully raised and the halyard cleated, the topping lift should be let out, which will cause the boom to drop slightly, which will flatten out the sail. The boom vang and mainsheet can be tightened again.

Since the boat is pointing into the wind, it's easiest to start sailing on a close hauled tack. You can use the motor to turn out of irons and then it should be cut off. You're sailing!

RAISING THE JIB

The jib should be deployed only after the main is up and the boat is sailing, and the process is fairly simple, whether for a furling or non-furling jib. We'll assume that the jib shackles are hooked to the forestay if the jib is non-furling. Also it is assumed that the jib sheets are already rigged to run through the fairlead and back to the cockpit.

For a non-furling jib, the sail is simply raised using the jib halyard. The wind fills the sails and the leeward jib sheet is used to set the sail. To prevent the sail from flapping uncontrollably and pulling the jib sheet out of the blocks, the leeward jib sheet can be pulled in slightly prior to raising the jib.

To unfurl a furling jib, the process is even simpler. The furling line is uncleated, but kept taught, and the leeward jib sheet is taken in as the furling line is slowly released. This action unfurls the jib, which immediately fills with wind.

LOWERING THE SAILS

Lowering the sails basically involves carrying out the sail hoisting procedure in reverse order. First the jib is lowered or furled, then the main.

The jib can be furled anytime. The boat does not necessarily need to be pointed into the wind, but heading on an upwind tack or being in irons will help the jib furl tighter and more neatly. Keep tension on the active jib sheet, slowly releasing it while brining in the furling line. When the jib is completely furled, the furling line can be cleated.

To bring down a non-furling jib, a crew member needs to go to the bow and pull the jib down by hand, bunching it up. Another crew member should uncleat the jib halyard and release it slowly as the jib is brought down. Also, the jib sheet should be let out slowly, but this can be done after the sail is down if there aren't enough crew hands to let out the halyard and the jib sheet at the same time. Once the jib is down, it can be held in place temporarily using bungees, to be stowed below deck upon return to the dock.

When lowering the main, it helps to point the boat into the wind, and in some cases the boat can be positioned so that a hill or tall building on shore blocks the wind to make things easier. Similarly to the jib, one crew member slowly lets down the halyard while another pulls the sail down by hand. As the sail is lowered, the bungees or straps used to hold it to the boom are replaced.

This process is best done with one crew standing forward of the mast, bringing down the sail, one crew lowering the halyard, and another wrapping bungees around the sail as it comes down.

Obviously, when fewer crew are available, it's a bit more hectic.

SETTING AND TRIMMING THE SAILS

SHEETING ANGLE

As discussed earlier in the section on wind forces, the primary variable used to control the sails is the sheeting angle, which in combination with the boat heading controls the sail angle of attack with respect to the wind. The sheeting angle is controlled by – you guessed it – the sheets.

The mainsail has only one sheet connected to the boom and some point in the cockpit. Since this sheet is connected to the boom behind the mast and stays, it is free to move back and forth and only one sheet is needed to control the angle of the boom.

The jib however has two sheets that wrap around either side of the boat. Since the jib is in the front of the boat, its sheets must be guided around the mast and side stays. If only one sheet were used, it would get caught on the mast when the jib flips from one side of the boat to the other. So for the jib, there are two sheets, both attached to the clew of the jib but fed around opposite sides of the boat.

Only one jib sheet actively controls the jib at a time. On a starboard tack (the wind coming over the starboard side of the boat) the jib sheet on the port side is used to control the sheeting angle and the starboard side jib sheet is loose. When the boat changes tack to a port tack, the formerly active (port) sheet is let loose and the opposite (starboard) is brought in to control the sheeting angle.

SHAPE

The shape of the sail – its twist and draft – can also be controlled to some extent. The jib shape is controlled primarily by the location of the fairlead, and the mainsail shape is controlled by the traveler. Moving the fairlead aft or the traveler windward will tend to flatten the jib or mainsail, respectively.

If you find that the mainsail has excessive twist or draft, it is most likely due to one or more of the following:

1. The boom vang is too loose
2. The topping lift is still engaged
3. The main halyard is not fully brought in
4. The clew outhaul is too loose

Items 1 – 3 lead to the mainsail being held too loosely in the vertical direction along the mast, while item 4 leads to looseness in the horizontal direction along the boom. Any such looseness will lead to excessive twist and draft.

TELLTALES

Over time, you'll develop a feel for the adjustments that need to be made to the sail. Small adjustments to the sheeting angle or sail shape will cause the boat to seem to "lock in" and accelerate. However, before you develop this instinct – but also when you're an experienced sailor – **telltales** are useful for determining the most efficient sail trim.

A telltale is a small piece of yarn, nylon, or other light line attached to the sail – or sometimes the stays – that indicates the wind flow at that point.

Telltales may alternately be called **yarns**, **wools**, **streamers**, or **tufts**.

Most useful for trimming the sails are the two telltales attached to either side of the sail near the luff and one attached to the leech. Typically, telltales on the port side of the sail are red and those on the starboard side are green (much like lights, as we'll see later).

Figure 14 illustrates how to react to different telltale behavior. When the sails are set properly, the telltales should be running parallel to the sail face on both sides of the luff and at the leech. When the sheeting angle diverges from its most efficient setting, the telltales begin to flutter on one side of the sail.

In general, to correct a misaligned sail, the sail should be brought towards the fluttering telltale. This correction can be made by either adjusting the sheet or changing the boat heading. For example, when the telltales are fluttering to windward, the sheet can be brought in (to harden up the sail), or the boat can be steered away from the wind (to fall off).

The luff and leech telltales can also be used in isolation. For example, sometimes the luff telltales may look good, but the telltale at the leech may be fluttering. In this case, only the leech of the sail needs to be adjusted. To make this adjustment without affecting the leech, the shape of the sail needs to be changed. A windward fluttering leech telltale would call for more curvature (draft) and vice versa.

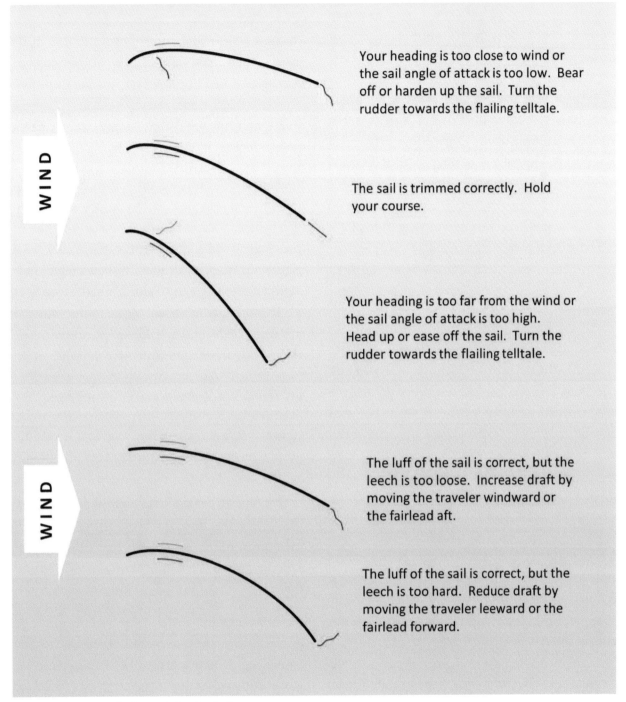

Your heading is too close to wind or the sail angle of attack is too low. Bear off or harden up the sail. Turn the rudder towards the flailing telltale.

The sail is trimmed correctly. Hold your course.

Your heading is too far from the wind or the sail angle of attack is too high. Head up or ease off the sail. Turn the rudder towards the flailing telltale.

The luff of the sail is correct, but the leech is too loose. Increase draft by moving the traveler windward or the fairlead aft.

The luff of the sail is correct, but the leech is too hard. Reduce draft by moving the traveler leeward or the fairlead forward.

Figure 14: Using Telltales to Trim the Sails

COMMANDS

The commands and terminology for communicating between captain and crew were been alluded to earlier in Figure 4. To **harden up** or **sheet in** is to bring in the sheet to reduce the sheeting angle. On the other hand, the captain instructs the crew to let out the sheet by telling the crew to **ease off** or **loosen up** the sail. While these commands are somewhat intuitive, and using them effectively certainly makes things run more smoothly, they aren't much help if your crew doesn't know what they mean.

OPERATING WINCHES

A winch is a spool-shaped device used to aid in bringing in the sheets on larger boats. The sheet is wrapped around the winch, which is cranked using a detachable handle connected to the top. The winch is made to turn in only one direction and the handle acts like a socket-wrench in that it can be moved back and forth and will only "catch" in one direction. It can also be spun 360°, but short back-and-forth movements give the most leverage.

To load a winch, the sheet is wrapped three times around in the active direction (usually clockwise). The sheet can still be pulled in by hand and the winch will spin freely. When the sheet becomes difficult to bring in further, the winch handle can be attached and cranked while tension is kept on the sheet. When the sail is trimmed, the sheet is cleated behind the winch.

Some winches are "self-tailing" which means there is a cleat built into the top of the winch. These make things easy by automatically keeping tension on the sheet while the winch handle is used, and by eliminating the need for the cleat behind the winch.

To loosen up the sails using a winch, the sheet can simply be uncleated – but not unwrapped from the winch – and let slip slightly until the desired sheeting angle is achieved, at which point the sheet is cleated again.

REEFING AND FURLING THE JIB

The best way to deal with strong winds is to avoid sailing when winds are dangerously strong, as discussed earlier. However, if you do find yourself in high winds, you will need to reduce sail area to prevent the boat from being overpowered.

Reefing is the process of lowering the main partway and tying it down to reduce sail area in high winds. The process is similar to that of lowering the sail all the way, but it is usually more difficult and dangerous since it is done under high winds. Accordingly, it's safer to reef too early at the first sign of dangerous winds, rather than too late when high wind and waves make controlling and moving around the boat more difficult.

The safest way to reef the mainsail is to sail on a close hauled starboard tack, and use the jib to power the boat while the mainsail is let out slightly to luff. The starboard tack establishes right of way, and the rigging used for reefing is usually on the starboard side of the boat. When the main is let out, it can be lowered slightly and tied off using reefing lines and reefing knots (how appropriate), described later in the section on knots.

The procedure for reducing the sail area of the jib is exactly the same as found in the section on raising and lowering the sails. Either the jib is brought down and a smaller jib is raised to replace it, or the jib is furled partway and the furling line cleated so that a smaller portion of the furling jib is exposed.

STEERING A SAILBOAT

Maybe you've heard the phrase "It's not like driving a car. It's like driving a boat." If you sail a few times you will understand exactly what that means. You might even start using the phrase yourself after you see how perfectly the analogy applies to so many real life situations. The bottom line is that boats respond much more slowly than cars, and when they do respond, they can be very difficult to control at all.

Since most people are accustomed to driving cars, they may try to turn a boat and expect something to happen. But it doesn't, at least not right away. So this initial delay leads to a tendency to overcorrect or turn too far. We will discuss more differences between boats and cars in the section on maneuvering under motor, but the moral of the story is this: make small adjustments when steering a boat – smaller than you think you need – at least when you're a beginner.

TILLERS AND WHEELS

Steerage of a sailboat is controlled by the rudder, which is mounted near the back of the boat. To put it another way, the rudder controls the back of the boat, which moves in the opposite direction of the front of the boat during a turn. So to turn the boat to starboard, the rudder is used to send the stern to port.

A tiller controls this rudder action directly – the tiller is simply a long lever attached to the top of the rudder – so to turn the boat starboard, you move the tiller to port. This action is often counterintuitive and takes some getting used to.

On the other hand, some boats have a wheel, which is connected to the rudder through a system of gears. The wheel is set up to turn the rudder in a manner that will guide the boat in the same direction that the wheel is turned. So when you turn a wheel to starboard, the gears turn the rudder to port (which you will most likely not even notice) and the boat turns to starboard.

To summarize, a wheel is designed to operate more intuitively like a car – you look where you want to go and turn the wheel that way – while tillers function in a somewhat counterintuitive manner – you move the tiller opposite to where you want to go.

Another way to look at it is that a tiller controls the direction of the stern while a wheel controls the direction of the bow. When moving backwards, it's just the opposite – a tiller controls the bow direction and a wheel guides the stern direction. However, just as when going forward, you move the tiller opposite the direction you want to move and a wheel in the same direction that you're aiming. The only difference is that you are now guiding the boat backwards.

LEEWAY

Earlier we discussed the fact that a portion of wind forces tend to push the boat sideways – technically abeam. Most of these forces are reacted by the hull, keel and rudder, but not all of them. So when you sail a boat perfectly straight along a certain tack, the side forces cause the boat to drift slightly downwind. **Leeway** refers to this sideways motion downwind.

It's important to keep leeway in mind when projecting your movement ahead. If you ignore leeway when attempting to sail around an object – as I have done more times that I care to admit – you will end up either coming too close for comfort, having to tack at the last minute, or worse, hitting the object.

The amount of leeway is dependent on the strength of the side force – which depends on the tack – and the ability of the hull, rudder, and keel to react those side forces. For a smaller boat that doesn't have a keel, it is important to use the centerboard to resist leeway, which is the main reason the centerboard is dropped further down as the boat approaches a close hauled tack (as seen earlier in Figure 9). In fact, the centerboard adds minimally to stability, but does a decent job reducing leeway.

HOLDING A COURSE

When you're sailing on an upwind tack, you'll notice that the wind seems to pull the bow of the boat into the wind. Usually the mainsail of a boat is larger in area than the foresail, so more of the wind force act on the back of the boat, pushing the stern away from the wind and turning the bow into the wind. So to hold a tack you'll need to keep turning slightly away from the wind.

Water waves, on the other hand, tend to act on the bow when you are sailing against them – and against the wind. So the waves tend to turn the boat away from the wind, at least on the front side of the wave. On the back side of the wave, gravity tends to make the boat fall back the other way. To hold a tack in heavy seas, you'll need to turn the rudder back and forth turning into the wind – and waves – on the front side of each wave and quickly correcting back the other way on the downside of the wave.

As we've seen, a sailboat cannot sail directly into the wind. The "no-go" zone covers approximately 45° on either side of the wind, so how does a sailboat move toward a desired point that is located upwind? The answer is by **tacking** back and forth on a zigzag-like path.

While the tack of a boat refers to its direction with respect to the wind, tacking refers to the action of turning into the wind so that the bow of the boat passes through the wind. With such an action, the sails are "flipped" to the opposite side and the boat assumes a tack on the other side of the wind. For example, a boat tacks from a close-hauled starboard tack to a close-hauled port tack. Note that the word tack is used to describe both the heading and the action of turning.

A sailboat can also turn so that the stern of the boat passes through the wind. This action is known as a **gybe**. The boom and sails are flipped to the other side of the boat for both a tack and a gybe, but the distinction is whether the boat is turning into or away from the wind.

A tack is illustrated in Figure 15 while a gybe is shown in Figure 16. Although these two actions may seem like the same thing – in fact, both are generally termed **coming about** – there are some key differences that need to be kept in mind.

First, the sails, and the boom are much further extended during a typical gybe than a typical tack. Although it is possible – and sometimes advisable – to tack from a port broad reach to a starboard broad reach by tacking 300° into the wind, most

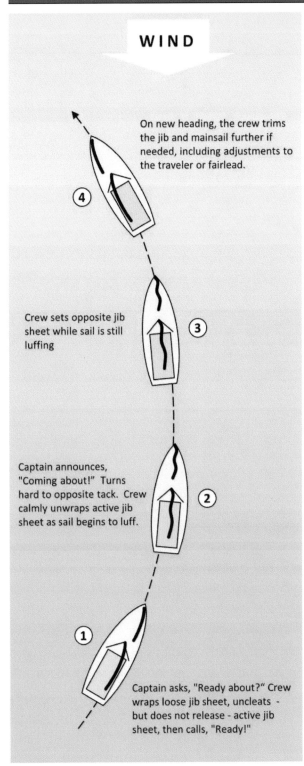

WIND

On new heading, the crew trims the jib and mainsail further if needed, including adjustments to the traveler or fairlead.

④

Crew sets opposite jib sheet while sail is still luffing

③

Captain announces, "Coming about!" Turns hard to opposite tack. Crew calmly unwraps active jib sheet as sail begins to luff.

②

①

Captain asks, "Ready about?" Crew wraps loose jib sheet, uncleats - but does not release - active jib sheet, then calls, "Ready!"

Figure 15: Tacking Procedure

gybe between close-hauled tacks, but there is no reason to ever do so intentionally. The sheeting angle is larger on downwind points of sail, the only circumstances for a gybe, so the boom travels a much further distance relative to the boat during a gybe than a tack. This difference can easily be seen by comparing the sheeting angles (the angle between the sails and the boat) in Figure 15 and Figure 16.

Second, the boom swings much more rapidly during a gybe than a tack. Notice from the figures that a tacking boat passes through the no-go zone, causing the sails to luff as the boat turns. The wind gradually fills the sails as the boat comes out of the tack. On the other hand, during a gybe, with the wind coming from behind the boat, the boat does not pass through the no-go zone, and the wind pushes the sails from fully extended on one side of the boat to fully extended on the other side of the boat nearly instantaneously. In fact, the wind can so easily change sides of the sail when the boat is pointing downwind, a gybe can even accidentally on runs.

These two factors, the distance and the rapidity of boom travel add up to a gybe being much more violent than a tack. This can be dangerous to the boat, and more importantly to the people aboard. Large forces created by the boom swing can cause wear and tear on the mast and rigging, and can also cause injury – potentially severe – if the boom comes in contact with someone's head. For this reason, the danger to the boat and crew, some charter companies forbid running, and you also might consider a similar moratorium on downwind sailing in high winds.

often such a turn is accomplished by gybing 60° away from the wind. Conversely, it is possible to

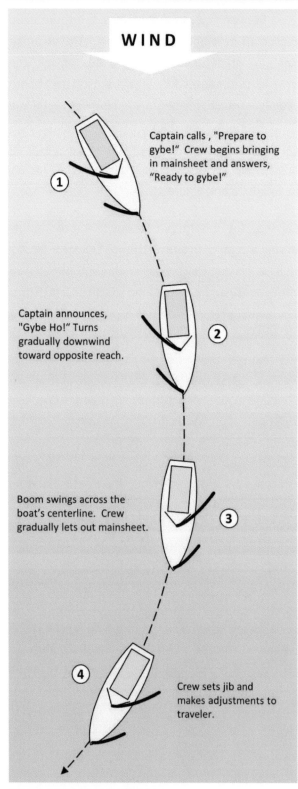

WIND

① Captain calls, "Prepare to gybe!" Crew begins bringing in mainsheet and answers, "Ready to gybe!"

② Captain announces, "Gybe Ho!" Turns gradually downwind toward opposite reach.

③ Boom swings across the boat's centerline. Crew gradually lets out mainsheet.

④ Crew sets jib and makes adjustments to traveler.

Figure 16: Gybing Procedure

TACKING PROCEDURE

Now that we've described tacking and gybing, we'll cover the actual procedure of each. Figure 15 gives the procedure for executing a tack. Note that the steps are described in terms of the captain's actions and those of the crew. On a single-manned sailboat, obviously, the captain would have to also carry out the crew's actions, and the communications wouldn't be necessary.

First, the captain announces the intention to tack by calling out "prepare to come about," or "ready about?" The crew then prepares for the tack by uncleating – but not releasing – the active jib sheet. The sheet is held in place by hand, and kept wrapped on the winch if one is being used. If there are enough crew, one person can get in position on the opposite side of the boat near the other jib sheet. Once in position and prepared, the crew lets the captain know by calling out "ready about," or "ready."

Next, the captain shifts the rudder or wheel hard to turn the boat across the wind towards the opposite tack, while announcing, "coming about" or "helm is alee." As the bow turns, the jib luffs and the crew releases the active jib sheet by simply letting go or calmly unwrapping it from the winch.

While the jib is still luffing, the crew sets the opposite jib sheet – wrapping it around the winch if one is used – and cleats it.

After the boat has reached the desired heading, the mainsail and jib can be trimmed further. The crew can make any remaining adjustments to the jib sheet and the traveler can be adjusted for the mainsail. Notice that no adjustments to the mainsheet are necessary for a simple tack to the opposite point of sail.

There are a couple things that can go wrong with a tack, both relating to working the jib sheets. If the active jib sheet is released too soon, the boat will lose power and may not have enough momentum to make it through the entire turn. Since the boat is turning through the no-go zone, momentum is critical for maintaining headway and steerage. If the jib sheet is released too soon, or the turn is not sharp enough, the boat can end up in irons.

Another possibility is that the opposite jib sheet is not set quickly enough by the crew. If the jib sheet is not set while the jib is luffing, it can become difficult to bring in the sheet with the sail full of wind. In this case, the captain can turn back into the wind slightly, allowing the jib to luff and making it easier for crew to work the sheets. Just be sure not to turn too far back into the wind and end up in irons.

GYBING PROCEDURE

The gybing procedure, shown in Figure 16, is similar to a tack. The main difference is that the mainsail is the focus of a gybe while the jib is the focus of a tack. To reduce the danger of the boom swinging across the boat, the mainsheet is brought in as the boat turns and then let out after the wind fills the sail on the other side. This reduces the boom travel at the moment that the wind switches from one side of the sail to the other, which greatly reduces danger.

The captain announces the intention to gybe by asking the crew to "prepare to gybe." The crew then responds by getting in position to work the mainsheet and announcing "ready to gybe."

The captain then begins to turn the boat – more gradually than during a tack – announcing "gybe ho" or "helm is aweather." The crew must then bring in the mainsheet as the boat begins to turn.

Once the boom swings across the boat – hopefully not very far since the mainsheet has been brought in – the crew begins to let out the mainsheet. When the gybe is complete, the crew can set the jib and make any remaining adjustments to the mainsheet and traveler.

Notice that the jib is not adjusted until the end of the gybe. Since the boat is not turning through the no-go zone as in a tack, there is no need to worry about losing momentum. The main concern is the danger of the boom swing. In racing situations or when more crew hands are available, the jib can be worked during the turn, but it's not necessary for making the turn.

PREVENTING AN ACCIDENTAL GYBE

The potential danger of an accidental gybe, as mentioned earlier, can be reduced by avoiding sailing directly downwind on a run. Another rule of thumb involves monitoring the angle between the bottom of the jib and the horizon. When the bottom of the jib falls so this angle is less than 45°, it's an indication that you may be getting too close to a run and an accidental gybe is possible. Adjust by heading up a bit towards a broad reach point of sail.

GETTING OUT OF IRONS

If you do end up in irons, you can simply wait until the wind and current pushes you one way or the other and you're able to fill your sails again. You can also speed things along by turning the rudder hard to one side. The wind will tend to slowly push the boat backwards and turn you in the opposite direction as you'd move if you had headway. The process can be helped along further by holding the jib on the opposite side of the boat. Figure 17 illustrates this procedure for getting out of irons.

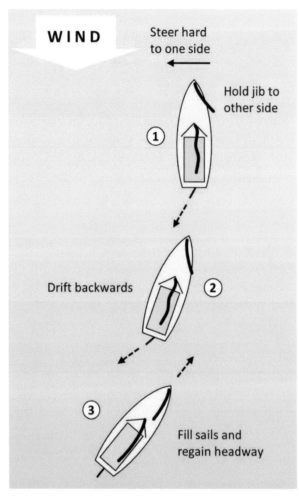

Figure 17: Getting Out of Irons

MAN OVERBOARD PROCEDURE

The man overboard drill is perhaps the most important skill you should know as a sailor. What's the second most important skill? Teaching your crew the man overboard drill so that if you should fall overboard, they can get you back in the boat!

Figure 18 illustrates the procedure for rescuing a man overboard (MOB). Essentially the idea is to steer onto a beam reach, tack around to the opposite broad reach, and come up downwind of the MOB.

If someone should fall overboard, the first step is to let everyone on board know about it by shouting out "Man Overboard." This should be done by the first person to notice that someone's fallen in the water. It's important not to lose sight of the MOB (which can be surprisingly difficult, particularly in rough weather). Ideally, one or more crewmembers can be assigned to do nothing but keep sight of the victim. If none are available, note the position of the MOB and maintain visual contact as continuously as possible.

As soon as possible after the MOB touches the water, throw him personal floatation device (PFD). If you've followed the pre-sail checklist, one will be readily available, with a long line connecting a throwable PFD to the boat's stern. If you're lucky, the MOB can get hold of the PFD and you can **heave to** while you pull him in. If not, you'll need to continue with the rest of the rescue procedure. At this point, you should either throw a second PFD that's not tied to the boat, or untie the rope connecting the PFD that's already in the water.

If the MOB cannot be rescued immediately using the throw line, the next step is to steer onto a beam reach while uncleating the jib. Letting the jib free does two things: It reduces boat speed, and it eliminates the complication of dealing with the jib sheet during the tacking and turning coming next. Note that it is not important which beam reach (90° or 270° to the wind) you steer to. Whichever is more convenient will work.

You may have to adjust the mainsheet, but the benefit of the beam reach is that the adjustment will be small no matter what point of sail you were on when the MOB fell into the water. In many cases, you won't have to adjust the mainsheet at all. Remember, the goal here is not to set the sail at its most efficient trim, just to control the boat and get the MOB back on deck. If you were on a close hauled tack, you'll probably want to let the main out a bid to prevent the wind from knocking you sideways, but otherwise, you may not need to adjust the main at all.

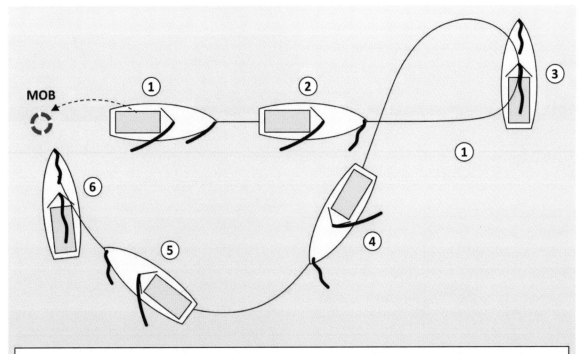

1. Throw PFD, call "Man Overboard," and note the position of MOB. Do not loose visual contact with the MOB.
2. Fall off onto a beam reach, uncleating the Jib.
3. At about 2 to 3 boat lengths from the MOB, *tack* into the wind onto the opposite beam reach.
4. Fall off onto a broad reach to get downwind of the MOB.
5. Turn up towards the MOB, naturally causing the sails to luff and boat speed to be reduced. Aim to run over victim as you straighten out into the wind
6. As the bow passes the MOB, turn away from him, causing stern to move toward him. Pull the MOB over the side of the boat opposite the boom. Or if necessary, use a boat hook or line to bring the MOB around to stern.

Figure 18: Man Overboard Procedure

Continue on a beam reach until you are 2 to 3 boat lengths from the MOB, always maintaining visual contact. Then tack – yes TACK – into the wind, all the way around onto the opposite beam reach. Then you will fall off a bit onto a broad reach. The first instinct of many sailors here is to gybe since that would be the usual way to get from a beam reach to the opposite broad reach. *Do not attempt to gybe!* Tacking here eliminates issues like boom swing and the jib wrapping around the forestay. Again, the goal here is not speed. It is safety and simplicity – particularly because you may be alone at the helm if your only crew is in the water.

Now, heading on a broad reach to a spot below the MOB, you can slowly turn up with the goal of being fully into the wind by the time you hit the MOB. The key element of this maneuver is that you don't have to adjust the sails. Turning up into the wind will naturally cause the sails to luff. You should have enough momentum to get to the MOB just as you are fully parallel with the wind.

As you approach, aim directly for the MOB, trying get as close as possible with the MOB on the side of the boat opposite the boom. On a larger boat, you may lose sight of the MOB as you get closer. When the bow passes the MOB, turn slightly away from the MOB, causing the stern of the boat to move towards the MOB.

It may be easiest to pull the MOB over the side (gunwale) of the boat on smaller boats. On larger boats you may need to use a boat hook or line to grab the MOB, at which point you can bring the MOB around to the stern to use the ladder.

HEAVING TO

Unfortunately, helming a sailboat requires constant attention. Some mechanical or electronic autopilot devices exist, but these are typically either expensive or of limited usefulness. Fortunately, there is an option for when the captain must leave the helm and there is no crew available to substitute.

Heaving to is a maneuver that putts the boat in a sort of holding pattern. By setting the sails and rudder in this configuration, the boat can be held in a stable position so the captain can leave the helm to attend to another task – e.g., reefing the sails, taking shelter from a storm, bringing in a MOB, etc.

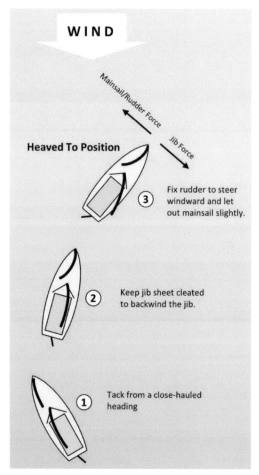

Figure 19: Heaving To

Basically, the jib is intentionally **backwinded** on an upwind tack – tending to turn the boat away from the wind – and the rudder is set to turn the boat into the wind – counteracting the jib. This configuration holds the boat steadily on a heading without any needed adjustments or attention from the captain. Since the mainsail also counteracts the jib, the net wind forces are minimal. The boat is not propelled forward and only drifts sideways slowly.

The procedure for heaving to, illustrated in Figure 19, is fairly simple. From a close hauled heading, simply tack without uncleating the jib sheet. Once the jib is backwinded and the mainsail is full, turn the boat hard back into the wind. The wheel or rudder can be fixed in position using a spare line.

The mainsail can then be let out slightly to reduce side forces on the boat, but should not be let out so far as to cause it to luff. The boat should remain in a stable position, without any further adjustments to the sails or rudder.

To get out of the heaved to position, simply turn the rudder back leeward to guide the boat ahead and uncleat the jib sheet. The mainsail will generate enough force to begin to propel the boat and the opposite (leeward) jib sheet can be brought in and set.

SPINNAKER HANDLING

One of the most beautiful and majestic experiences in sailing is using the spinnaker, also known as the "chute" or "kite." You may have had the chance to see a picturesque ocean horizon filled with the colorful teardrop shapes of distant spinnakers. If so, it will be tough to resist the urge to "fly the chute" whenever the opportunity presents itself.

Unfortunately, the spinnaker can only be used under certain conditions. As mentioned previously, the spinnaker functions only in drag, so it cannot be used when sailing upwind. The spinnaker is only useful on a beam reach and below.

Since the spinnaker is so large, it should only be used in light to moderate winds, or there is a real risk that it will overpower the boat. Remember, you deal with strong winds by reducing sail area, which is counter to the huge sail area of the spinnaker.

On the other hand, there needs to be enough steady wind to be sure that the spinnaker will be filled at all times. Since the spinnaker is not fixed along one or more edges like the other sails (the mainsail is fixed along the boom and mast, the jib along the forestay), it can easily become tangled and difficult to handle if it's not always filled with wind.

The fact that the spinnaker has more "moving parts" means it's more difficult to operate than the other sails. It's best to have at least three competent crewmembers aboard, including the captain, when using the spinnaker. You'll need one person to helm the boat, one to work the sheets and one to work the spinnaker rigging on the foredeck.

A lot can go wrong with the spinnaker. In strong winds, the spinnaker can overpower the boat, causing loss of control and knockdown danger. For this reason, *stop knots should never be tied in the spinnaker sheets*. It's important that the sheets can be let free quickly under an emergency and stop knots are counter to that aim.

Less dangerous mishaps involving the spinnaker are more common. The spinnaker can be twisted on itself forming an hourglass as both the top and bottom sections fill with wind. This embarrassing and annoying problem can occur either when the sail is raised improperly, or if the spinnaker is not kept full of wind.

If close attention is not paid to the rigging, spinnaker sheets can become tangled in the stays or lifelines. If the halyard is attached to the wrong corner of the sail, it can be raised sideways, the ultimate embarrassment.

SPINNAKER RIGGING

Due to the aforementioned lack of connection to the forestay, spinnaker rigging is slightly more sophisticated than the other foresails. The halyard, as usual, is connected to the head and used to raise and lower the spinnaker. Each bottom corner of the spinnaker is connected to a line whose name changes based its relationship to the wind at the moment. The leeward of these two lines is called the sheet, while the windward is called the **guy**.

A **spinnaker pole** is connected to the mast and the corner of the sail controlled by the guy. The pole holds the spinnaker away from the mast and provides some stability to the sail shape (without the pole the spinnaker would have too much draft). The topping lift and **downhaul** are connect to the end of the pole by the **bridle**, or ring, and are used to control the angle of the pole.

Ideally, the spinnaker is stowed in a pouch attached to the deck or lifelines that facilitates raising and lowering the sail. These operations are easiest if done with the pouch on the leeward side of the boat.

FLYING THE CHUTE

Here's the basic procedure for deploying the spinnaker. It is assumed you are sailing with a mainsail and jib, and that you're sure the conditions are appropriate for spinnaker use as described above.

1. **Sail onto a broad reach.** Note, this doesn't necessarily need to be done first. It can be done any time prior to raising the spinnaker halyard. However, since a broad reach is a fairly calm tack and there will be some work on the foredeck to be done, I suggest taking this step first.

2. **Check the spinnaker for twists.** With the spinnaker still stowed in its pouch or bag, pull all three corners out of bag. Follow each edge of the sail from corner to corner to find and correct any twists. Ideally, this process can be done on shore prior to sailing.

3. **Rig the spinnaker sheets.** Attach the halyard, sheet and guy to the appropriate corners of the sail (the head should be clearly marked). When flying, the spinnaker should end up in front of forestay and outside everything else on the boat, so make sure to rig the lines to the outside of the forestay, sidestays, lifelines, etc. Again, *do not tie stopper knots in the spinnaker sheets* as that could be extremely dangerous in high winds.

4. **Rig the spinnaker pole.** Attach the spinnaker pole to the mast and connect the topping lift and downhaul. Adjust the topping lift and downhaul so that the pole is level. Connect the spinnaker pole to the windward corner of the spinnaker (note this will bring the spinnaker out of its bag a bit, so be ready to get it up as soon as possible after this step).

5. **Raise the spinnaker.** Hoist the sail by bringing in and cleating spinnaker halyard.

6. **Set the sheets.** Set spinnaker by adjusting the sheet and guy. The sail should be directly downwind, acting entirely in drag.

7. **Trim the spinnaker.** Once the spinnaker is in a generally good position, cleat the guy and use only the sheet to make any minor adjustments. One indicator of proper spinnaker trim is the bottom of the sail, which should be level with both clew and tack at the same height. Another indicator is the curl (or draft) of the sail which should give it some fairly good shape. Never let the spinnaker become to flat or it may stall.

8. **Drop or furl jib.** This step can be taken any time after the spinnaker is raised, but it's best to wait until the spinnaker is fully set to avoid confusion and make best use of limited crew.

TRIMMING THE SPINNAKER

Again, the spinnaker is trimmed by using the sheet only, with the guy only adjusted when gybing or making significant heading changes. The pole angle and the spinnaker curl have already been mentioned as trim indicators, but we'll reiterate them here and add some further details:

1. **Spinnaker pole height.** The pole should be level and set so that the tack and clew of the sail are also level. Pole height is

affected primarily by the topping lift and downhaul.

2. **Sheeting angle.** The sheets should be set so that the spinnaker pole is perpendicular to the wind. The angle of the spinnaker pole is determined by the guy.

3. **Sail shape.** The spinnaker should have significant draft, and it will naturally curl simply due to its shape and rigging. The general guideline of a flatter sail in stronger winds applies, but the spinnaker should never be too flat or it will stall. To increase draft, ease the sheet.

GYBING WITH THE SPINNAKER

Gybing with the spinnaker is slightly more complicated than a normal gybe since the spinnaker pole needs to be flipped manually from one side of the sail to the other. However, it's not too difficult if done properly. Here are the basic steps:

1. **Sail directly downwind.** Trim the spinnaker for a dead run. If you're on a broad reach, you'll ease the sheet, and bring in the guy. Keep a close watch on the boom – all the dangers of gybing still apply. Steering the boat during a spinnaker gybe is as simple as keeping the boat directly behind the spinnaker, almost like you're following the spinnaker. This will take you on an S-like curve and keep the spinnaker in a stable position relative to the boat, allowing the crew to easily set up the rigging. Make sure before you gybe that you have enough room around you to complete the

process, i.e., you don't want to be in close quarters or surrounded by other boats.

2. **Gybe the main.** You'll first turn slightly past a dead run towards the opposite broad reach to gybe the main – intentionally so it doesn't happen by accident. Then you'll turn back downwind to a dead run. See the S-like path coming into play?

3. **Flip the spinnaker pole.** One crewmember will go to the foredeck and change the spinnaker pole to the opposite side. It's not as simple as just allowing the pole to rotate like the boom. First, detach the end of the pole from mast and attach that end to the opposite corner of the spinnaker (now both corners of the spinnaker are attached to the pole). Then, detach the pole from the other corner of the sail and attach that end of the pole to the mast. Now the former sheet is the guy, and what was the guy is the sheet.

4. **Steer onto the new broad reach** and trim the sails as necessary.

LOWERING THE SPINNAKER

Just like the other sails, lowering the spinnaker is accomplished by essentially reversing the sail raising procedure. Here's an outline:

1. **Steer to a broad reach.** As with raising the spinnaker, it's easiest on a broad reach.

2. **Raise or unfurl the jib.** You'll want the jib up once the spinnaker is down. Raising it

first shields the spinnaker from the wind, making handling easier. You can now steer the boat deliberately to where the jib blocks the most wind from the spinnaker.

3. **Detach the spinnaker pole and guy.** One crewmember will go forward to take this step, then gather in the bottom of the spinnaker (foot) while the sheet is let out slowly under tension, similar to furling the jib.

4. **Lower the halyard.** Once the foot of the spinnaker has been gathered, the spinnaker can be pulled down while the halyard is released.

5. **Re-stow spinnaker and rigging.** When stuffing the spinnaker into its pouch or bag, be sure to keep it free from twists so it can be easily raised next time.

MOB WITH THE SPINNAKER

Since the spinnaker can only be used when sailing downwind, the normal MOB procedure is impossible with the spinnaker up. The spinnaker makes a serious situation even more dangerous.

To pick up an MOB, the first step is to get rid of the spinnaker, by either dropping it quickly using the normal procedure, or by simply cutting the lines and letting it fly away. The danger of the situation needs to be judged in real-time to determine if there's time to drop the spinnaker, with the safety of the MOB as the first priority.

If the situation calls for it, let the spinnaker go by uncleating the sheet and guy and letting them run free. The halyard will have to be cut. If there is enough time, you can tie a lifejacket to one of the sheets and try to recover spinnaker after picking up the MOB.

If you judge the situation to be less serious, simply lower the spinnaker as in the normal procedure and then proceed with the MOB recovery. The only difference from the normal spinnaker lowering procedure is that you don't need to fly the jib, since extra power is not what you're after during an MOB recovery.

MOORING AND ANCHORING

MOORING PROCEDURE

A **mooring** is sort of like a permanent anchor. It is simply a buoy that is weighted to the seafloor that you can hook your boat up to. Most marinas that are heavily trafficked by temporary visitors have moorings. Be sure to check the procedure for using a mooring prior to your visit. You don't want to use a mooring that it owned by someone else. Usually there's a radio channel for the marina that you can call for information and getting a mooring assignment.

You might want to drop your sails and motor into a mooring (if so, see the section on handling under motor), but you can also approach while under sail. It is very similar to picking up an MOB. You want to approach on a beam reach from beneath (leeward) the mooring and turn up into the no go zone so the sails luff and you have just enough momentum to carry you to the mooring. To reduce power, you should either drop the jib or let the jib sheets run free like in the MOB procedure. It's a bit tricky since you want to be sure you have enough momentum to get you to the mooring, but you don't want to run it over.

There should be a line or chain, called a **pendant**, permanently attached to the mooring. Grab it with a boat hook and tie one of your dock lines to it and a bow cleat.

When the boat is hooked up to a mooring, it will naturally drift downwind in the absence of a strong current. So to leave the mooring, you'll first need to head back toward the mooring to detach your line. You can do this by either pulling on the line, or if you're on a larger boat, by motoring or sailing up to the mooring. Of course, sailing is the most difficult since you'll be heading directly into the wind and you won't have much room, if any, to maneuver.

Once you're detached from the mooring, you can motor away, or follow the steps for getting out of irons described earlier.

ANCHORING PROCEDURE

Anchoring a boat is a bit more precarious than tying up to a mooring. If you don't know what's on the seafloor, it's easy to get your anchor stuck, or **fouled**. It can also be illegal to anchor near coral reefs or other marine habitats. For these reasons, it's best to avoid anchoring if possible, but if you must, follow these steps:

1. Find a suitable spot. Muddy bottom is best, and large rocks are the most likely candidates to foul your anchor. The water should be shallow enough so that the length of your anchor line is at least 7 times the depth of the water. You can find out the seafloor condition and depth either using a chart, checking visually, or by dropping a **lead line**. Be sure to take into account the fact that winds may change, which may cause you to rotate

about your anchor. You don't want to drift into other boats, land, etc.

2. Moving backward slowly, drop your anchor. Make sure the anchor line is tied to the **bitt** and it is not tangled up on any lines, stays, or most importantly your foot!

3. Take the engine out of gear and drift backward, letting out the anchor line until at least 7 times the depth of the water is out. Then tie off the line to a bow cleat. You should feel the anchor grab the seafloor with a significant, jarring halt.

4. Note your position using either visual landmarks or your electronic navigation system, to be sure you do not drift.

To raise the anchor, motor slowly to the spot directly above the anchor, bringing in the line as you proceed. If your anchor is stuck, the best chance you have to free it is by making large circles around the spot.

REACTING TO STRONG WINDS

As I've stated before, the best way to avoid dangerous winds is to stay ashore. However, if you do find yourself in the middle of rough winds, there are several ways you can minimize the danger.

The quickest and easiest way to react to strong winds is to simply let the sheets out a bit, even to the point of letting the sails luff. However, you should avoid luffing the sails for an extended period of time as it may cause damage to the sails.

As we discussed earlier in the sections on sail trim, flattening the sails is a good way to respond to stiff winds. If you're on a boat with a centerboard, drop it completely, as this will make the boat easier to control.

You can also increase stability by falling off a bit. As we've learned, lateral stability is lowest on a close-hauled tack, so falling off provides a flatter, calmer ride.

If winds begin to overpower the boat, you should respond by reducing sail area. This can be accomplished by reefing or furling the sails, or switching to smaller jib (there's a reason it's called the storm jib). The next step is to drop one of the sails entirely. Many larger boats – i.e. cruisers – are controlled well with the jib only. However, using the mainsail only can make handling the sheets easier. The best option depends on the boat and needs to be found through trial and error.

If you still find yourself unable to control the boat at all, drop both sails and ride out the storm. If you're on a cruiser, you're likely to at least have motor power, but in rough seas, that might not help much either. Dropping anchor may be an option if you have enough line to allow for the ebb and flow of the swells. An alternative to dropping the sails is the heave to position which can also be used to ride out a storm.

Generally it is best to go to shore if dangerous winds are approaching, but once winds reach a certain strength, it's actually safer to stay away from shore and ride out the storm (see the Beaufort Wind Scale above). This same idea applies to dropping anchor. While it can stabilize you in moderate winds, the anchor can cause more problems than it solves in very strong winds.

When things get rough, remember to putt on a life jacket, wear harnesses if available when going onto the foredeck, and stow or secure anything that doesn't need to be on deck (get your vegetable platter out of the way!).

Of course, the best option is always to avoid rough whether by keeping a close eye on the forecast and calling it quits at the first sign of danger.

SMALL SAILBOAT TACTICS

So far, this book has mostly focused on cruisers, i.e., larger, more stable boats that have a keel and keep you fairly dry under most conditions. If you should choose to sail on smaller boats from time to time for practice or the occasional thrill, there are a few special tactics that you'll need to know.

For our purposes, a small sailboat is defined as one without a keel such as a racing dingy, or a small catamaran. Basically, a boat that will fit one to two people and will get you wet, whether you fall into the water or not. Side note: be sure to always wear a life jacket aboard a small sailboat.

As we've discussed previously, the side forces created when sailing at angle to the wind are offset primarily by the keel, if the boat has one. On smaller boats without a keel, you have to be much more proactive to limit the two effects of side forces: heeling and leeway.

USING THE CENTERBOARD AND RUDDER

The primary means of limiting leeway on a smaller boat is using the centerboard. As we've alluded to earlier, the centerboard can be dropped partially or fully, depending on the point of sail.

Some boats have a centerboard that drops straight down through a slit in the bottom of the boat, while others have a centerboard that is permanently attached but rotates at an angle from fully up (parallel to the bottom of the boat) to fully down (perpendicular). Either way, the concept is the same.

The rudder also resists leeway, and some boats have a rotating rudder, much like the latter centerboard configuration just described.

However, the main purpose of this type of rudder is to prevent it from getting stuck in the sand when launching from a beach. So don't worry about fidgeting with the rudder depth while sailing. Just drop it all the way down once you leave the beach and leave it there until you're going back ashore.

As you might expect, the centerboard should be dropped progressively further as the side forces increase, i.e., as you sail closer to the wind. Notice in the points of sail chart (Figure 9) that the centerboard is fully dropped on a close hauled tack, halfway down on a beam reach, and completely raised on a broad reach.

That said, it's usually better for the centerboard to be too low than too high. Controlling the boat while sailing into the wind will be more difficult with the centerboard up. When sailing downwind however, the only real consequence of dropping the centerboard further than necessary is the added drag. Unless you're racing, or the winds are very light, this additional centerboard drag probably won't bother you too much. If you've got plenty of wind and aren't trying to set any speed records, you can just drop the centerboard down all the way and forget about it.

TRAPEZING OR HIKING OUT

The other effect of side forces, heeling, is controlled on small boats primarily by shifting the weight of the crew. Since there is no keel, and the boat is lighter overall, the boat is highly sensitive to the location of the crew. You will immediately notice the boat rocking if you move from one side to the other. On smaller boats, you will constantly have to shift sides and body position.

To limit heeling and prevent the boat from capsizing, the first step is to shift all crew topside, i.e. the windward side of the boat that is lifting out of the water. Leaning backwards partially over the side of the boat will further increase righting forces.

In heavier winds the weight of the crew needs to be shifted out past the edges of the boat to limit heeling. In this process, known as **trapezing** or **hiking out**, the crew hang over the edge of the boat. While strapped to a line connecting them to the mast to prevent them from falling into the water, the crew basically stand on the edge of the boat and lean backwards to maximize righting forces.

Trapezing is a fairly advanced skill, and beginner sailors should avoid going out when winds are strong enough to make trapezing necessary. However, but if you have the necessary equipment (straps, lines, and harnesses) and don't mind getting wet, it is quite exhilarating.

LAUNCH AND RECOVERY UNDER SAIL

Launch and recovery of small boats are different from cruisers in two important ways:

1. There is no motor power.
2. The sails – or at least the mainsail – is up before you leave.

Accordingly, you need to use sail power to guide you away from land, and you need to be aware of sail forces even when you are stationary. The sail – or sails – will initially be free when you're stationary, and you'll need to set them at a carefully chosen sheeting angle to start sailing.

When raising sails while ashore, use the same general procedure, but make sure the sheets are somewhat loose (but not completely free) and the sails are pointed into the wind. You don't want the sails full until you're out on the water.

If you're familiar with the sailing concepts and maneuvers we've discussed so far, you can probably piece together the methods of launch and recovery without a motor. But we'll walk through them just to be clear.

If you're launching from a beach, there should be either an onshore or offshore wind (see the section on coastal wind patterns). Figure 20 and Figure 21 show the steps for launching from shore.

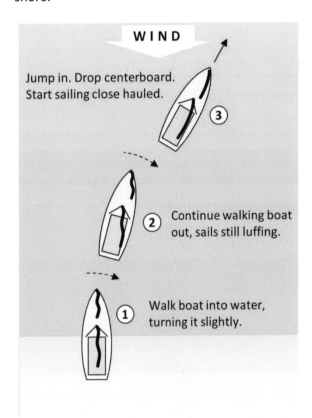

Figure 20: Launching into the Wind from Shore

Notice that you'll always start with the bow pointed into the wind. The idea is to start with the boat in irons with the sails luffing so you can control the boat when walking it out into the water.

When you're launching into the wind, you simply turn the boat a bit as you walk it out, jump in, and start sailing on a close-hauled tack. Dropping the centerboard as soon as possible improves control.

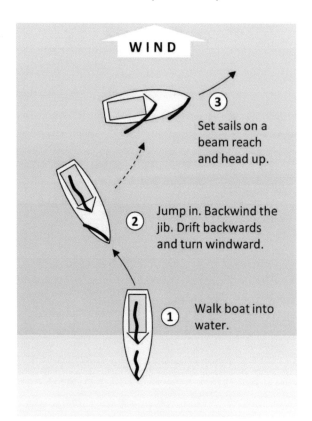

Figure 21: Launching with the Wind from Shore

You may notice that launching against the wind is very similar to the procedure for getting out of irons. You manually hold the jib into the wind to push the boat backward and rotate around. When you're about perpendicular to the wind, you can set the sails on a reach and head up quickly to get away from shore.

The launching procedures from a dock (shown in Figure 22 and Figure 23) are basically the same as from shore, but you have the added benefit of a fixed object (the dock) to push off of. Start by walking the boat out to the end of the dock using a **dock line**. Then follow the same procedure as when launching from shore.

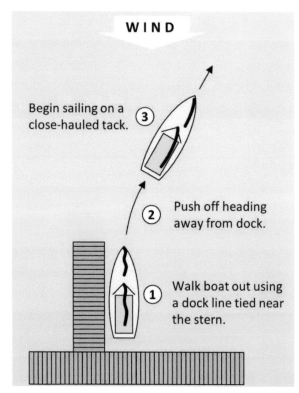

Figure 22: Launching into the Wind from a Dock

Recovery under sail can be a bit more difficult simply because you can't always finish with the boat facing into the wind. For example, when sailing into the shore with the wind at your back, as shown in Figure 24, you will go ashore with full sails. For this reason, it's best to drop the mainsail while you're still on the water. That way you don't have to worry about an accidental gybe. You can heave to and drop the mainsail, or if you have enough hands on deck, just follow the normal procedure for dropping the main. Once the mainsail is down, you can sail to shore on a broad reach, ending on a run. As soon as you reach the shore, drop the jib.

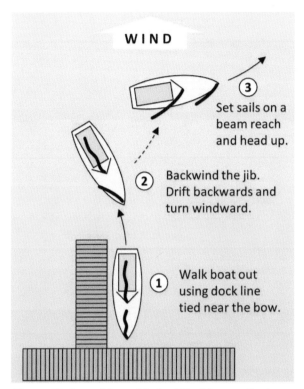

Figure 23: Launching with the Wind from a Dock

Recovering against the wind, illustrated in Figure 25, is nearly identical to the end of the MOB procedure. Simply turn up into the wind from a reach and use your momentum to reach shore while the sails luff. If the wind is very strong, you can let the jib run free to slow down, just as in the MOB procedure.

Docking with an onshore wind is a bit trickier. Since you want to end up pointed into the wind, you may have to sail very close to the dock on a beam reach and head up at the last minute, as shown in Figure 26.

Another alternative is to simply follow the same process as for going ashore, i.e. approach on a

run. However, if you choose the latter option, dropping the mainsail away from the docks is a must, and you need to be very careful not to ram the dock. Whenever you are recovering with strong winds, be sure to let the sheets out a little further than normal, to dump some wind power.

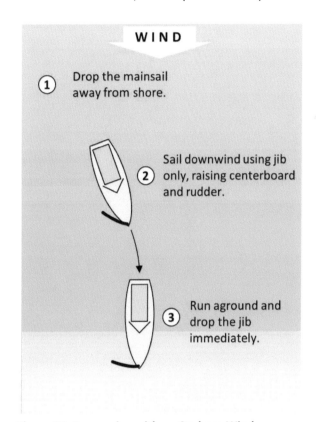

Figure 24: Recovering with an Onshore Wind

Figure 27 shows the process for docking into the wind, which is exactly the same as sailing ashore into the wind. The only difference is the harsher consequence of coming in too fast. Sand is soft and forgiving, while docks are not. Be very careful that you don't have too much momentum coming into the dock.

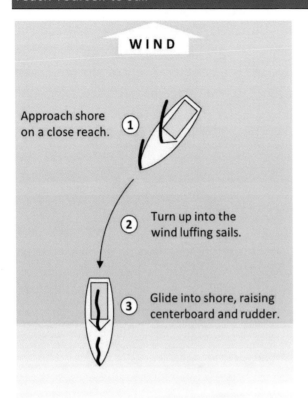

Figure 25: Recovering into an Offshore Wind

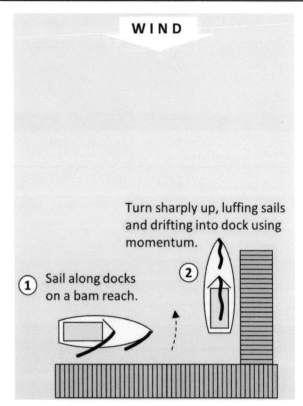

Figure 26: Docking with an Onshore Wind

There is also one possibility we haven't discussed. The wind will usually be coming from either onshore or offshore when you are launching and recovering from a beach. However, docks are not always aligned with the shore as shown in the previous figures. You may encounter a situation where you must dock with the wind coming perpendicular to the dock. In that case, you'll need to sail on a beam reach close to the dock and then head up into the wind when you get close to the spot you want to dock. At that point you can backwind the jib and drift slowly backwards into the dock.

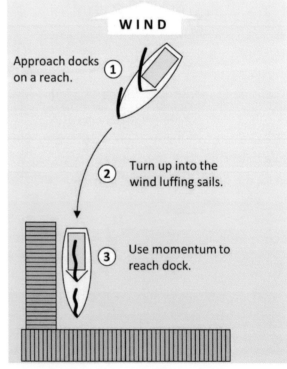

Figure 27: Docking into an Offshore Wind

CAPSIZE RECOVERY

Since they lack the righting force of a keel, small boats are much more easily capsized. You can reduce the likelihood of capsizing by only sailing in light winds and learning to hike out in stronger winds. Even so, capsizing is inevitable if you sail smaller boats often. Fortunately, unlike keelboats, which are virtually impossible to right after being capsized, small boats, can be recovered readily.

To recover a small dinghy, take the following steps:

1. Let all sheets run free. This will prevent the boat from sailing away with you still in the water once it is righted. Keep track of the mainsheet however. You'll need it immediately after righting the boat.

2. Grab any cargo that fell overboard – such as spare life jackets – and put it in the cockpit. On some small boats, the rudder can come loose easily, so be sure that it is secure before proceeding.

3. Move to the bottom side of the boat. Pull down on the centerboard, and if necessary climb onto it and grab the beam. Use your weight to pull the boat upright.

4. When the boat is upright and you are still in the water, pull in the mainsheet (ever so slightly) as you lift yourself into the boat over the beam. This will give the boat a bit of headway and prevent you from pulling it over on top of yourself when you get in.

MOTORBOAT TACTICS

You may be wondering why, in a book on sailing, there is a section on motorboat tactics. Well, when a sailboat is powered by a motor, rather than its sails, it is a motorboat. This point may seem trivial, but it's an important distinction (as we'll also see in the discussion on right of way rules).

In fact, motoring in and out of the marina can be the most perilous and nerve-racking skill a recreational sailor must master. Once a sailboat is out on the water, there's plenty of room to maneuver, and getting thrown off course a bit is no big deal. In the marina however, you aren't so lucky. Everywhere you look, there are hazards: other boats, docks, channel walls, etc.

I've seen **slips** where there is as little as six inches on either side of the boat. Imagine backing out of that slip, trying not to bump the dock with the side of the boat, watching for other boats coming through the channel behind you, and all the while knowing the charter company you rented the boat from can't wait to fine you for the slightest scuffs you cause to the boat.

Too many recreational sailors, me included, focus on sailing techniques, without paying enough attention to how to actually get out of the marina first. The good news is that if you understand the basics of motoring, you'll be able to handle it without any issues.

MOTORS AND PROPELLERS

A motor drives a boat by turning a propeller which displaces and redirects water underneath the boat. Much like our earlier discussion of wind aerodynamics, this movement of water creates forces that are reacted by the boat, propelling it through the water. The movement of the propeller primarily creates a flow of water directly behind the propeller, known as **prop wash**. Similar to sailing against the wind, a less desirable side force, called **prop walk**, is also created as a byproduct.

INBOARD VS OUTBOARD MOTORS

There are basically two types of motors used on sailboats, inboard and outboard. An outboard motor hangs over the transom and can be turned just like a rudder (using a handle that acts like the tiller). Outboard motors steer the boat by directing prop wash, replacing the rudder. In fact, when using an outboard motor, the rudder should be taken out of the water.

Inboard motors, on the other hand, are housed inside the boat. Only the propeller protrudes from under the boat, just forward of the rudder. The propeller is in a fixed position, always directing the prop wash straight aft. The direction of the boat is controlled by the rudder moving through the water (or sometimes the prop wash acting on the rudder), but not by the prop wash direction alone, as in an outboard motor.

This distinction is the important contrast between inboard and outboard motors. Inboard motors rely on the rudder to control the boat, prop wash only acting to propel the boat forward, but not to change its direction. Outboard motors use prop wash to control the boat directly. Accordingly, outboard motors provide greater maneuverability. However, since most larger boats use inboard motors, it's important to understand how to operate inboard motors as well.

FUELING

Filling up your gas tank on a boat is slightly more complicated than your car, but not by much. The main dangers of fueling are fire and carbon monoxide poisoning. Common sense will reduce these dangers. Don't smoke or have any open flames or sparks when fueling. Keep enclosed spaces well ventilated by opening windows, hatches, etc. Follow the Coast Guard's fuel safety checklist (Figure 28) and you should have no problems.

FUELING SAFETY CHECKLIST
Prior to Fueling
1 Close all doors, hatches, and ports.
2 Turn off all electrical equipment.
3 Extinguish all open flames.
4 Turn off galley stove and heaters.
5 DON'T SMOKE!
6 Instruct crew and passengers on safe practices. (Consider having passengers go ashore during refueling.)
After Fueling
1 Open doors, hatches and ports.
2 Operate blowers for at least 4-5 minutes.
3 Clean up all fuel spills.
4 Check all compartments by "sniffing" for fuel fumes.
5 Have a fire extinguisher at hand for engine start.
Source: US Coast Guard

Figure 28: Fueling Safety Checklist

ENGINE CONTROLS

Controlling a boat engine takes some getting used to. Typically, inboard engines are controlled by two levers. One lever switches between gears – forward, neutral, and reverse – while the other level adjusts the engine speed.

As you can imagine, operating these two levers, plus the wheel, takes some coordination, and can be tough if you're in a tight spot and aren't completely sure what you're doing. All the more reason to become comfortable with the concepts and maneuvers covered in this section and practice whenever you have the opportunity.

CAVITATION

When you find yourself in a tight spot, drifting the wrong way, the first impulse is to crank up the throttle to try to change direction. More often than not, this doesn't help. Either the boat doesn't respond in the way you expect, or it doesn't respond at all. All you hear is a high pitched whine. Unfortunately, if you rev the engine too quickly, you can cause a phenomenon called cavitation.

When the propeller moves too quickly through the water, small bubbles form all around the propeller face. When these bubbles pop, tiny water jets impact the propeller, causing damage. And of more immediate concern, the propeller basically spins freely, through the air bubbles, not creating any prop wash to drive the boat.

Cavitation is most likely to occur when the propeller is close to the water surface, which is easy to prevent with an outboard motor. Just make sure the propeller shaft is dropped as far into the water as possible. With an inboard motor, there's not much you can do to change the propeller depth.

Usually cavitation is rare unless the engine is too powerful for the propeller size. Just be aware, if you hear a high pitched squeal, your propeller is not doing the work you're intending. Ease off the throttle a bit, and if possible, drop the propeller deeper into the water.

CONTROLLING THE BOAT UNDER MOTOR

As we alluded to earlier in the discussion on inboard vs. outboard motors, a motor boat is controlled primarily by redirecting the thrust of the propeller, or prop wash, either by directly turning the propeller shaft on an outboard motor or by using a rudder on an inboard motor. Prop wash, the side force byproduct of propeller spin, can also be used constructively. Figure 29 illustrates the propeller forces created by an inboard motor in forward gear.

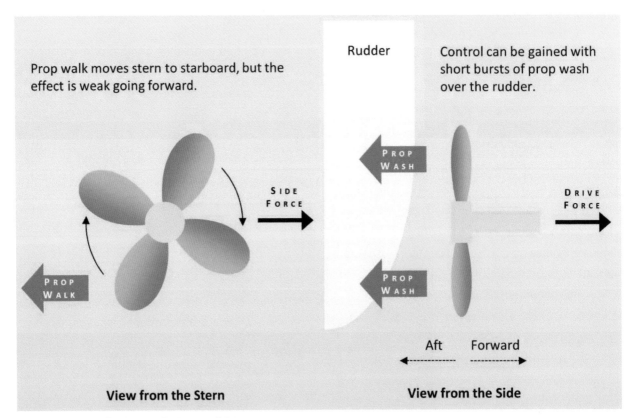

Figure 29: Propeller Forces in Forward Gear

Unfortunately, the rudder is only effective when the boat is travelling forward, or there is a large burst of prop wash. This fact is the main reason that maneuvering a boat in tight quarters is tricky. There are no brakes, and you need to be moving to have any control at all using the rudder.

A rule of thumb for delicate maneuvering is to use the *minimum power required to maintain rudder control*. There's no need to go any faster, but go any slower, and you'll be at the mercy of the current and wind.

Prop walk on the other hand, does not require headway, but it is much more pronounced when the propeller is going in reverse (see Figure 30). This, and the fact that it acts perpendicular to the boat, makes prop walk ideal for making sharp turns. However, it only acts in one direction, so it must be used carefully.

Prop wash, can also be effective without headway, but only in short, strong bursts. A burst of power creates a quick jet of water that can be redirected sharply by the rudder to create a side force, similar to prop walk. Since the rudder is aft of the propeller, this method only works with the engine in forward gear.

Accordingly, one method for turning sharply is to alternate between quick forward and reverse engine burst to take advantage of both prop walk and prop wash, as we'll discuss later.

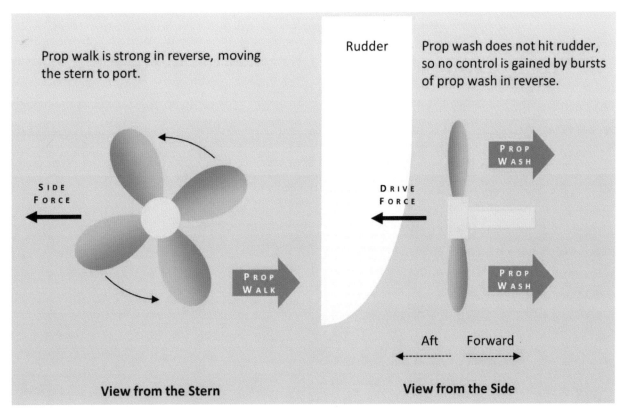

Figure 30: Propeller Forces in Reverse Gear

WIND AND CURRENT

Aside from the propeller and rudder, which you can control, there are also outside forces acting on the boat that you can't control. It's important to be aware of how wind and current will turn the boat, so that you can best counteract them or use them to your advantage.

Yes, wind will act on a boat even when the sails are down. The wind will push on the side of the hull – most prominently on the bow, since it has the highest profile – tending to turn the bow away from the wind. The current, on the other hand acts mostly on the stern, since it is the deepest part of the boat, turning the bow into the current.

It's difficult to predict which outside force, wind or current, will dominate. Suffice it to say that if you aren't actively controlling the boat using the propeller and rudder, one of these two forces will take over. Fortunately, while you're inside a marina, much of the current and wind will be blocked, but you should still keep them in mind when planning your maneuvers.

PIVOT POINT

One big difference between boats and cars is the **pivot point**, which is the point around which the object rotates during a turn. Figure 31 illustrates these differences. All boats are unique, but as a general rule, the pivot point on a sailboat is about one third of the way back from the point where the bow touches the waterline. The pivot point on a boat is the same whether you're moving forward or backwards.

A car's pivot point, on the other hand, depends on the direction, due to the fact that the car has two sets of wheels. When going forward, the pivot point is near the middle of the car, roughly even with the driver. When moving in reverse, a car's pivot point is between the rear wheels, behind the driver.

The "feel" of driving is determined by this relationship between the locations of the driver and the pivot point. So fundamentally, a boat feels different because the driver is located well aft of the pivot point, while on a car, the driver is right on top of the pivot point. Of course, that difference applies when moving forward.

When driving a boat backward it feels more like a car (going forward) because the pivot point is behind the driver (who's now looking backward). For this reason, it's sometimes more comfortable to move forward of the wheel when going backwards in a boat.

It's also important to understand the pivot point, because boats are much longer than cars. At the helm of a boat, you must always be aware of movement of both the bow and the stern. It's easy to be looking one way, behind the boat for example, focusing on the stern, and forget that the bow is swinging around behind you possibly colliding with a dock or another boat.

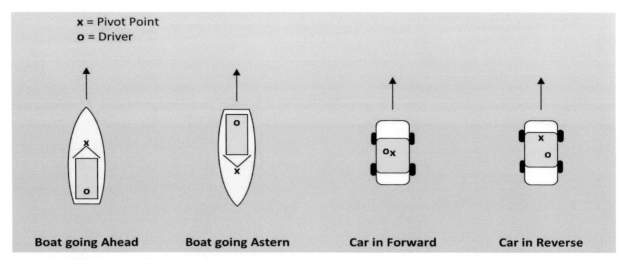

Figure 31: Differences in Pivot Point between Cars and Boats

COMMON MANEUVERS

The figures and most of the discussion in this section assume a standard "right-handed" propeller, which turns clockwise when going ahead and counterclockwise when going astern. For a left-handed motor, all directions will be reversed, but the concepts will still apply. The orientation of the propeller can be checked by driving it in reverse with the wheel and rudder pointed dead ahead. If prop walk moves the stern to port, it's a standard, right-handed propeller. If the stern moves to starboard, you've got a left-handed propeller.

For a normal, right-handed propeller, prop walk acts by pulling the stern to starboard when the engine is in forward gear. When in reverse, prop walk pulls the stern to port and is much more pronounced, as mentioned earlier.

When making sharp turns, prop wash can be used in short bursts to turn the bow either way. However, this action mainly rotates the boat, but doesn't move it forward.

To turn the boat while moving forward, normal rudder control must be used, which requires headway and more room to maneuver.

These considerations along with the ideas discussed earlier lead to some general guidelines for maneuvering under power, as summarized in Figure 32.

10 Tips for Maneuvering Under Power
1 Go only fast enough to maintain headway and steerage.
2 Always turn clockwise in close quarters.
3 Understand your boat's pivot point (typically 1/3 astern from the bow waterline). Be aware of BOTH bow and stern movement.
4 Wind turns the bow downwind.
5 Current turns the bow into the current.
6 Prop walk moves the stern to starboard going forward (but not significantly), and the stern to port going astern.
7 On a boat with a wheel, you can drive "like a car" when going astern by moving to the forward side of the wheel.
8 Put out your fenders when working in tight spaces. Hope to not use them, but be prepared.
9 Think about how you will correct if you overshoot or undershoot your turn. That will often determine the best path to take.
10 If you get into a tight spot, think about reversing your course and starting fresh, rather than trying to

Figure 32: Guidelines for Maneuvering Under Power

SHARP TURNS

The best way to turn the boat sharply in tight space is to use a combination of prop walk and prop wash to rotate the boat with minimal forward or backward motion. As shown in Figure 33, the rudder is set hard to starboard and held in that position. Then, the engine is alternated between short, powerful bursts in forward and reverse gear.

The forward bursts use prop wash to produce a quick thrust, turning the bow to starboard. The reverse bursts create a side force using prop walk that moves the stern to port. Both of these actions turn the boat in the same direction without much headway or sternway. The reverse bursts will produce some sternway, though minimal, so it's best to begin this maneuver with a bit of headway to avoid drifting too far backwards.

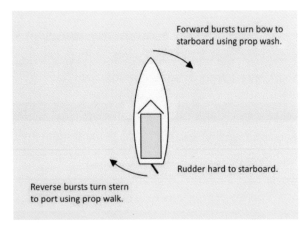

Figure 33: Sharp Turns

HOLDING A POINT

A similar method is used to hold a point, i.e. a heading, which may need to be done while mooring or taking down the mainsail. To hold a point, short forward and reverse engine bursts are used as above. Here however, the rudder is set hard to port (see Figure 34).

The reverse bursts still produce prop walk, acting to send the stern to port. The forward bursts, however, now send the bow to port, acting opposite the movement created by prop walk. In this position, you simply need to watch the bow and keep it pointed at an object in the distance (or into the wind using a wind vane atop the mast). When the bow moves too far to starboard, give the engine a quick forward burst. When the bow moves too far to port, give the engine a burst in reverse.

Again, there will be a slight tendency for the boat to drive backward, but this can be corrected by holding the engine in a forward gear with low power and moving forward slowly.

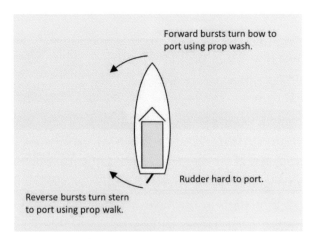

Figure 34: Holding a Point

LEAVING AND BERTHING

When leaving and **berthing** a slip, you have very little room to maneuver and must end up in a spot not much wider than your boat. The more you can think through your maneuvers in advance, the more you will be prepared to correct from minor deviations without panicking.

Generally, you'll be backing out of a slip. A rare few boats will be berthed stern-in, but the concepts here can be adjusted accordingly without much difficulty.

The basic idea that you must keep in mind is that the boat can be turned much more sharply in the clockwise direction (see the section on sharp turns). Therefore, it makes most sense to turn that way when backing out of a slip. As you can see, from Figure 35 and Figure 36, you'll always begin by turning the stern to port once you clear the slip.

The next steps then fall into place based on which direction you need to go to exit the channel. When you're leaving a slip to starboard, you go forward upon completing the initial rotation.

When you're leaving a slip to port, you continue backwards until you have more room to maneuver.

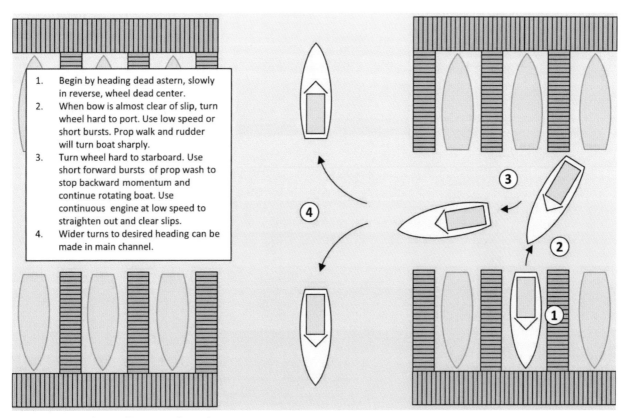

1. Begin by heading dead astern, slowly in reverse, wheel dead center.
2. When bow is almost clear of slip, turn wheel hard to port. Use low speed or short bursts. Prop walk and rudder will turn boat sharply.
3. Turn wheel hard to starboard. Use short forward bursts of prop wash to stop backward momentum and continue rotating boat. Use continuous engine at low speed to straighten out and clear slips.
4. Wider turns to desired heading can be made in main channel.

Figure 35: Leaving a Slip to Starboard

When berthing to a slip, the sharp rotation to port is used only as a final corrective maneuver to slow down and/or sharpen the turning radius into the slip. When approaching a slip to starboard, as in Figure 37, you simply make a smooth, controlled turn into the slip, preferably in one motion. A turn that is too sharp can be corrected with bursts of reverse, which will swing the bow around to port. If the turn is too wide, there's no way to correct, because any reverse engine thrusts will cause prop walk, further exacerbating the situation. In that case, it's better to simply back

out of the slip as in the leaving procedure and head out to the main channel to start over.

When approaching a slip to port, you may be able set yourself up with the slip to starboard by reversing into the channel, as in Figure 38. In that case, once you're past the slip, you simply proceed as above tuning to starboard. Alternately, if there isn't room behind the slip, or you're simply not as comfortable going in reverse, you can approach the slip going forward turning to port. In this case however, prop walk is less helpful for making corrections. While logic would suggest that a turn that is too wide could be corrected with a burst of prop walk to swing the stern back to port, the bow is likely to have bumped the dock by that point.

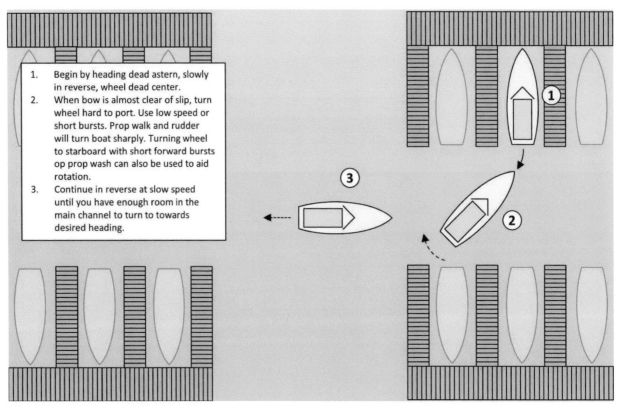

1. Begin by heading dead astern, slowly in reverse, wheel dead center.
2. When bow is almost clear of slip, turn wheel hard to port. Use low speed or short bursts. Prop walk and rudder will turn boat sharply. Turning wheel to starboard with short forward bursts op prop wash can also be used to aid rotation.
3. Continue in reverse at slow speed until you have enough room in the main channel to turn to towards desired heading.

Figure 36: Leaving a Slip to Port

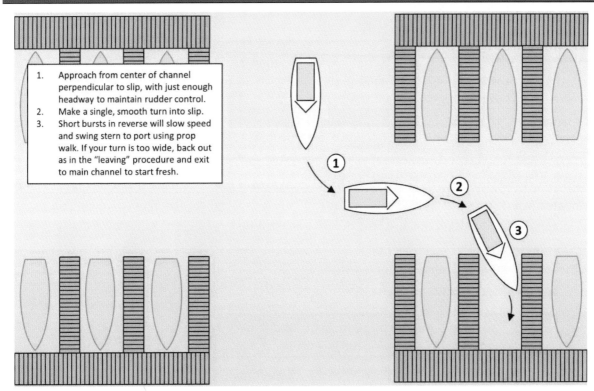

1. Approach from center of channel perpendicular to slip, with just enough headway to maintain rudder control.
2. Make a single, smooth turn into slip.
3. Short bursts in reverse will slow speed and swing stern to port using prop walk. If your turn is too wide, back out as in the "leaving" procedure and exit to main channel to start fresh.

Figure 37: Berthing a Slip to Starboard

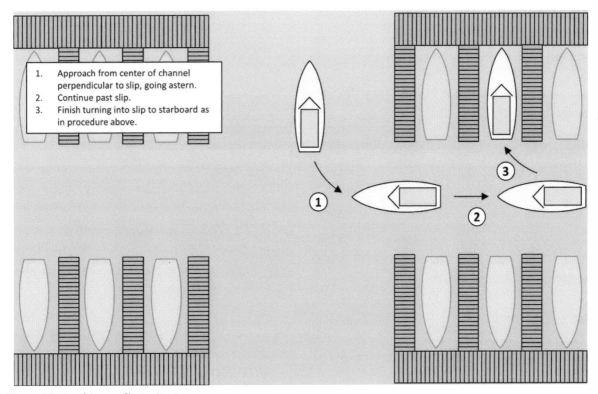

1. Approach from center of channel perpendicular to slip, going astern.
2. Continue past slip.
3. Finish turning into slip to starboard as in procedure above.

Figure 38: Berthing a Slip to Port

GENERAL SEAMANSHIP

Any time you go out on a watercraft, there are certain things you should know, regardless of the type of boat. This section covers information that's not specific to sailing, but that you'll need to know if you're going to be a sailboat captain.

LAWS AND REGULATIONS

As a boater, you must abide by both federal and state boating laws. The purpose of this book is not to be a comprehensive legal reference, so I'll only point you to the appropriate resources for learning about each set of laws.

Federal boating regulations are summarized by the US Coast Guard (USCG) in various courses and references. The most convenient that I've found is a printable pamphlet offered free online by the USCG. It also gives an overview of a lot of the other material – not necessarily legal requirements, but good practice nonetheless – covered in this section. Here's the link:

http://www.uscgboating.org/assets/1/workflow_staging/Publications/420.PDF

Each state has different boating laws, so you'll need to find the appropriate reference for your state. For example, some states require a license to own or operate certain classifications of boats, while others do not. The USCG has a nice online resource that compares boating laws of each state, which can be found here:

http://www.uscgboating.org/state_boating_laws.aspx

To find a more complete reference, just do a simple Google search for your state, e.g., "CA boating laws."

SAFETY

LIFEJACKETS

Lifejackets – or more generally personal floatation devices (PFDs) – are classified by their function and buoyancy into five types. Figure 39 describes each type.

Federal law requires at least one lifejacket (any non-throwable type) per person to be on board any boating vessel. Larger boats (16 ft or longer) additionally require at least one throwable PFD. More information on PFD usage is provided by the USCG online at:

http://www.uscgboating.org/safety/life_jacket_wear_wearing_your_life_jacket.aspx

On smaller sailboats, it is good practice to wear a lifejacket at all times, rather than just have one on board to meet the legal requirement. The likelihood of falling into the water in the course of normal boating – as opposed to only in an emergency – is fairly high.

On larger sailboats, particularly those with lifelines, you don't need to *wear* a lifejacket unless the conditions are very rough, or you can't swim. Otherwise simply having a PFD aboard for each person and a throwable ready to deploy is safe enough since falling overboard is rare.

The throwable can be tied to a long line connected to the boat near the stern so it can be easily tossed from the cockpit during an emergency. If you've got your own boat, I

Type	Name	Minimum Buoyancy	Description	Usage	Example
I	Off-Shore Life Jacket	22 lb	Able to turn most unconscious adults face up into a breathing position.	All recreational and commercial vessels	
II	Near-Shore Buoyant Vest	15.5 lb	Able to turn most unconscious adults face up into a breathing position.	All recreational vessels	
III	Flotation Aid	15.5 lb	More sleek design for watersports	All recreational vessels	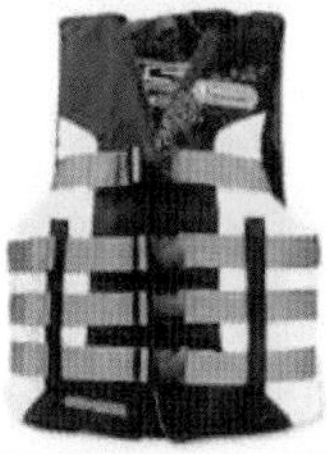
IV	Throwable Device	N/A	Designed to be thrown in emergency MOB. Rings, horseshoes, or seat cushions.	Required by law on 16+ ft boats.	
V	Special Use Device	Substitute for Types I - III according to label	Typically inflatable	Must be worn to count as legal	

Figure 39: PFD Classifications

recommend a product called the LIFESLING that serves this purpose. It's basically a throwable PFD with a line attached that's designed to be easily stowed and deployed.

OTHER SAFETY EQUIPMENT

Along with the Coast Guard PFD requirements already mentioned, most states require additional safety equipment on board boating vessels. Again, reference your specific state's boating laws to determine exactly what equipment is legally required, but the list is likely to include some combination of the following.

Navigation lights can be either built into the boat or can just be a simple handheld flashlight for smaller boats. They are typically required from sunset to sunrise or during any period of low visibility, i.e., fog. However, if you're only sailing during the day, and the weather is nice, you won't have to be too concerned with lights.

Some type of **sound signaling device** may be required as well. Specific requirements for the type of device usually depend on size of boat.

Carrying some form of **visual distress signal** may also be required. As with sound signally devices, visual distress signals vary widely in terms of sophistication, from a flags to a signal flares. The type of signal required is usually dependent on how far away from the coast you'll be sailing and the size of your boat.

If you're boat has a motor, a **fire extinguisher** should be on board, as is usually required by law, particularly with inboard motors. The fire extinguisher can be a handheld unit like you may have in your home, or often it is some sort of system that's built into the motor housing.

Other motor equipment such as a backfire flame arrestor, a muffling system, a ventilation system can also be required. Fortunately most motors meet these requirements by design, so it's not something you have to worry about.

If you are chartering a boat, all legally required safety equipment should be provided by the charter company, but you should always take inventory prior to casting off.

CLOTHING AND FOOTWEAR

It's always good to dress in layers when boating. The temperature on the water is usually significantly different than over land. Also cloud cover and wind speed can dramatically affect the temperature that you experience.

It's also good to bring towels and spare clothing in case you get wet. Usually the first step in hypothermia treatment requires drying off completely and getting into dry clothes. Obviously this requires that towels and change of clothes are available.

Footwear is also important aboard a sailboat. Boat shoes are designed to be non-slip and have non-marking soles. If you're going to wear shoes that aren't specifically designed for boating, be sure that they offer a good grip. Unfortunately, many types of shoes will mark up the boat with black scuff marks, which can be a real pain to clean off. Open toed shoes are also not recommended. There are plenty of toe-stubbing opportunities aboard a boat.

HYPOTHERMIA

A somewhat surprising fact about boating is that hypothermia is usually a bigger threat than drowning, particularly in chilly waters. Most people are aware of the possibility of drowning, but neglect the risk of hypothermia and therefore aren't adequately prepared to react to cold water immersion.

What is hypothermia?

Hypothermia is the condition that occurs when the body losses too much heat and begins to shut down. First, motor control of the limbs is lost, and eventually the rest of the body shuts down.

The victim loses the ability to speak, has difficulty breathing, loses consciousness, and eventually dies.

Hypothermia can occur in dry cold weather, but it happens much more quickly in wet conditions due to thermal conductivity of water being much higher than air. What makes hypothermia even more dangerous to boaters is that the process can continue even after a victim has been removed from the water, and therefore would seem to be safe.

Hypothermia Prevention

Cold water immersion can cause death surprisingly quickly. Lethal exposure times for several water temperatures are shown in Figure 40. Note how the lethal exposure time decreases dramatically as you expend energy either treading water or swimming.

Approximate Median Lethal Exposure Times			
	Time in Hours		
Water Temp (°F)	Floating with PFD	Treading Water	Swimming
35	1.75	1.25	0.75
45	2.5	1.75	1
55	3.5	3	2
65	7.75	5.75	4.5
70	18	13	10
			Source: US Coast Guard

Figure 40: Hypothermia Lethal Exposure Times

The takeaway is this: *if you do fall in the water, the best course of action is to conserve energy by staying in place and balling up to try to keep warm*, rather than making a hopeless attempt to swim for it. Obviously, you're also much better off if you've got a PFD.

Note also that these are average times for all different types of people. Those who are very old, very young, or in generally poor health will fare even worse. Use of alcohol or other depressant drugs also increases susceptibility to hypothermia.

Hypothermia Treatment

Suffice it to say that once any sign of hypothermia is observed, treatment should be sought immediately, and the victim's health should be monitored closely. The initial sign of hypothermia, rather than just "being cold" is the body beginning to "give in." For example, shivering stops and you don't really feel cold anymore, just tired and weak.

To treat a hypothermia victim – or a potential hypothermia victim, i.e. any MOB – dry off the victim, get him out of wind, and get him into dry, warm clothing. Warm food or drink can also help raise the body's core temperature. Radio for medical help immediately, and contact the Coast Guard if you believe the situation is life threatening (we'll discuss different types of distress calls later).

When considering whether or not to call for help, it's better to be safe than sorry. As mentioned earlier, the process of hypothermia, once set in motion, can continue even after you think you're out of woods. It's best to seek medical attention as early as possible.

SEASICKNESS

Seasickness is not as serious a condition as hypothermia, but it can spoil a fun day. Being seasick will also make a person more prone to hypothermia if they should be unfortunate enough to fall overboard as well. Some people are more prone to seasickness than others, but no one is completely immune. And even if you don't suffer from seasickness yourself, it's no fun to have to take care of someone who does.

Generally, those who are in a healthy, rested, and energetic condition are less susceptible to seasickness. Accordingly, alcohol, illness, and lack of sleep can all increase the chances of being seasick.

Prevention

Sometimes people who know they are prone to seasickness are able to take preventative measures, but success varies. Generally, anything that settles the stomach – e.g. carbonated drinks, ginger products, staying hydrated, getting fresh air, small frequent snacks rather than big heavy meals – can be used to prevent seasickness. Over the counter medications such as Dramamine are available, and more powerful prescription drugs can be obtained through a doctor.

Why Sailing is like Dancing

Most people get dizzy when they spin around in circles, but not experienced dancers. They manage to twirl around and around all day without the vomit-inducing sickness that we mortals would experience.

So how do they do it? Well, if you've ever watched closely or even taken a dancing class, you might notice that the trick is to control your eyes.

You pick a spot on the wall and focus on it, keeping your head and eyes still while the rest of your body turns. Just at the last moment, when the body has almost completed a full revolution,

and you can no longer hold your head still without breaking your neck, you whip your head around as quickly as you can and find same spot you were looking at. This action minimizes the disorienting dizziness that normally accompanies spinning around.

The mechanisms in your head that control balance and dizziness when you spin around also cause seasickness. So to fight seasickness, you must control your head, much like a dancer. One way to keep your head stable is to focus your eyes on something that is not moving, i.e., the horizon.

OK, that was a very long winded way of telling you to look at the horizon if you want to fight off an approaching bout of seasickness, but at least now you have a good story when you want to explain it to your passengers.

This – along with the lack of fresh air – is why the cabin is the worst place to be if you're prone to seasickness. Your view of the horizon is blocked, so you have nothing steady to focus on.

Another way to keep your head level is to stand up and hold on to something. By allowing your knees to bend, you can absorb some of the motion of the boat, keeping your head more stable.

The captain can minimize the motion of the boat by avoiding a heading that is perpendicular to the waves. All these actions are indented to achieve the same result: keeping your head as steady as possible.

KNOTS

You don't need to be an Eagle Scout to sail. There are entire books written on how to tie knots for everything from baiting a fishing hook to decorating your living room. Fortunately, there are a handful of knots that you can learn that will cover just about any situation you'll encounter while sailing.

ESSENTIAL KNOTS FOR SAILING

Figure 41 summarizes the knots that every sailor should know and their uses. They're all fairly simple and easy to learn. Detailed instructions for tying each type of knot are in the appendix.

Knowing how to **coil and hang a line** is essential for keeping lines that aren't being used out of the way. And of course, you'll need to know how to tie, or **belay**, a rope to a cleat. The **figure eight** knot is the only stopper knot you'll ever need.

You may need to tie your boat up to a post or hang a coil from a stanchion. For that you'll use a **clove hitch**. The **anchor bend** is another type of hitch knot useful for tying an anchor line, as the name would suggest, and for hanging fenders off of side rails. The **bowline** will create a loop in the end of a line that can be used in an MOB emergency as a grab line or as a step when lifting an MOB aboard. It's also great for tying a throwable PFD to a throw line.

If you ever need to connect two lines of different sizes, there's a knot for that. It's called the **sheet bend**. If you need to connect two lines of the same size, or two ends of the same line, while reefing for example, use a **reefing knot**.

Name	Usage
Coiling and storing a line	Storing lines loosely below deck or in other compartments.
Coiling and hanging a line	Hanging up lines on a hook or cleat when not in use.
Belaying a cleat	Fixing a line to a cleat. Most often a sheet to an onboard cleat, or a dock line to a dock cleat.
Figure Eight Knot (savoy knot, love knot)	A stopper knot tied in ends of cleats so they aren't accidentally pulled out of their blocks.
Clove hitch (pet knot, boatman's knot)	Tying a dock line to a vertical post during mooring. Hanging a coiled line on a horizontal stanchion.
Anchor bend (fisherman's bend, round turn and two half hitches)	A alternative to a clove hitch during mooring. Tying an anchor line to its bitt. Hanging fenders from vertical gunwale stanchions.
Bowline	Tying a line to an object, such as PFD or bucket. Tying a loop in a line to be used as a step or handle during MOB recovery.
Sheet bend	Joining two ropes of different sizes.
Reefing knot (square knot)	Tying reefing lines around the mainsail and boom. Joining two ropes of same size.

Figure 41: Essential Sailing Knots

PRACTICING TYING KNOTS

If you want to practice tying knots, there are all kinds of fancy knot tying kits for sale. They typically include some rope and a piece of wood with a post, a hook, and/or a cleat attached to it. If you really want to get serious about knots, go

for it. But the odds are that after you spend about 30 minutes with this thing, it's going to become another piece of useless junk lying around your house.

I recommend that you do what I did. Go to a superstore like Walmart or Target, and buy some round shoe laces, maybe two different widths so you can practice the sheet bend. Cut the tips off and used a match to **cauterize** the ends just like normal boat lines. You don't have to do this, and it won't work if the laces don't have wax in them, but it keeps the ends from fraying.

Now you have some miniature lines that you can use to practice the various sailing knots. Tie the lines together. Tie them to your oven handle, your coat hook, you get the idea. Another option is to go to a hardware store and buy some real line. It will be a bit more expensive than shoelaces, but less expensive than a knot tying kit.

When you're done with your makeshift practice lines, you can either throw them out, or make a decorative knot, such as the Monkey's Fist, and spice up your home décor with a new accent piece.

RULES OF THE ROAD

When two ships pass in the night (or the day), how do they avoid crashing into each other? In other words, how do they know who has the right of way? Who turns (**gives way**) and who just keeps on going straight (**stands on**)? The guidelines used to answer these questions are known as the **rules of the road**.

A TEACHING MOMENT

I was out sailing one day with a bunch of friends in the middle of the Santa Monica Bay. Beautiful day. Immaculate 36-foot bareboat-chartered yacht. My friend Dan spots another sailboat coming towards us off our port bow and warns me in a somewhat panicky voice, "Should we turn?" Seeing this as a teaching moment, I respond with the question, "Who has the right of way?"

Dan doesn't know the answer, so I explain, "We're on a starboard tack, so we have the right of way. Don't worry. He'll turn." As the distance between the boats closes, Dan becomes progressively more worried. I remain calm, comfortable in the fact that we're the stand on vessel, so the other boat will give way.

The other boat doesn't turn. We pass in front of him by about 20 yards. Not exactly a near death experience, but far closer than you ever need to get to another boat when it's just the two of you out on the wide open ocean. As we get close enough to cast a condescending glare at the other captain, I notice something strange: *no one is at the helm!* Just then, a head pokes out of the cabin and it becomes clear why the other boat didn't give way.

It turns out that it *was* a teaching moment, for *me*.

MY TWO GENERAL GUIDELINES

The first takeaway from my teaching moment is this: *never assume the other boat knows what it's doing*. Particularly when you are in an area with a lot of other recreational boaters, more often than not, the other captain is ignorant, drunk, just not paying attention, or all of the above. So be cautious and assume the other guy isn't going to turn.

The downside to not being able to rely on other boaters to know the rules of the road is that you lose the main benefit of the system: clarity. The whole point of having well established rules is to make sure everyone is on the same page.

You might have realized this, but communicating with another boat is difficult. Furthermore, when you have 360 degrees of available space to work with, your next move is not always clear to other boaters. The rules of the road provide clear guidance for how boats should behave to avoid collisions. So while you should not assume other boaters know the rules, your approach should be to follow them until it starts to become evident that the other boat is not.

That brings us to the second general guideline for encountering other boats. *When you make a move, make it obvious.* The other boats can't read your mind. If you decide you are going to adjust course to give way or avoid another boat, always make a large, exaggerated move – rather than just a small course adjustment – so that the other boat cannot mistake your intentions. Confusion can lead to a collision. If you are cautious, courteous, and make obvious moves to give way to other boats when possible, you may never come close enough to need the rules of the road.

THE RULES OF THE ROAD PROPER

The rules of the road are described in terms of right of way hierarchy in the following figures. Sometimes you'll see these are listed in opposite order ("A gives way to B" instead of "A has right of way over B"). Since I'm an alpha male, at least when I'm captaining a ship, I find them easier to internalize this way.

The first set of rules, listed in Figure 42, determine which boat has the right of way between different types of boats. For example, sailboats have right of way over motorboats, but not over fishing vessels.

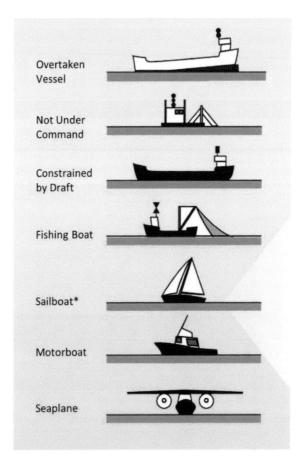

Figure 42: Rules of the Road Hierarchy

The right of way between two sailboats is determined by the wind and the tack of each boat, as shown in Figure 43. Two rules cover most situations. First, a sailboat on a starboard tack has right of way over one on a port tack. The tack, of course, is determined by the windward side of the boat (or alternately, the side opposite the boom). Second, when two boats are both on the same tack, the leeward boat has the right of way. Other situations arise, and are described in the figure, but these two rules cover most encounters.

When two boats under motor cross paths, the right of way is determined according to stand on and give way zones, as illustrated in Figure 44. These zones match lighting requirements, but they also apply during the day. The idea is simple. If you see a red light (or the red zone of a boat during the day), give way. If you see a green light, stand on. Two boats will never see green if they're on a collision course.

1. A sailboat on a **starboard tack** has right of way over one on a port tack.

2. If two sailboats are on the same tack, the **leeward** boat has the right of way.

3. A sailboat in the process of **tacking or gybing shall give way** to other sailboats.

4. If two sailboats are in the process of tacking, the **boat on the other's port side shall give way**.

Figure 43: Rules of the Road for Sailboats

The elegance of this system is that you only need to worry about what you see in front of you. You don't need to go through an elaborate logical process like, "OK, the other boat is pointing at my starboard bow, which is in my green zone, therefore he is going to stand on, so I need to give way." Instead, you just look at the other boat. Do you see green or red? That's all you need to know. You do, however, need to know the zones during the daytime even without the aid of lights, as mentioned earlier. Also, if you see the white zone, it means you are overtaking the other vessel, and need to give way.

When two boats meet exactly head on, they should determine their actions through sound signals, as discussed later, but the convention is that both boats turn to starboard.

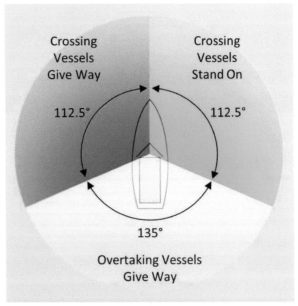

Figure 44: Stand on and Give Way Zones

SIGNALS AND COMMUNICATION

The Rules of the Road are essentially a way to replace the need for communication to avoid a collision. But sometimes, the conversation goes beyond "let's not run into each other."

One example already mentioned is sound signals, which are primarily used to communicate maneuvering intentions in tight spaces. Other types of signals include flags, lights, radio calls, and distress signals. If you're fortunate, you'll never have to use any of these, but you should have a basic understanding, and keep reference material onboard at all times.

SOUND SIGNALS

Sound signals can be made by either a horn that is built into the boat or a handheld air horn. There are two types of basic signals, a **short** and a **long blast**. A short blast is about 1 second and is sometimes called a **toot**. A long blast lasts around 4 to 6 seconds.

Communicating intentions increases safety any time there is a chance of collision, but is even more critical in conditions of limited visibility (i.e., fog). As already mentioned, when two boats meet head on, the convention is for both to turn to starboard, but relying on another boat to act and/or to know your intended actions is dangerous.

Figure 45 gives the meaning of basic sound signals. Note that there is a subtle difference between international/coastal standards and inland standards in the meaning of the action signals. The coastal convention is to signal your intention, wait for confirmation, then act. A signal is confirmed as received, understood, and agreed to by the receiving boat repeating the signal. Conversely, the inland standard is to signal your action as you are taking it, rather than to wait for confirmation.

Signal	Meaning
1 Short Blast	I am turning to starboard and/or passing you to port
2 Short Blasts	I am turning to port and/or passing you to starboard
3 Short Blasts	I am slowing down or backing up
5 Short Blasts	Danger, a collision is imminent
1 Long Blast	I am generally alerting other boats to my presence in restricted visibility (Any boat coming around a blind bend, or larger boats in the fog).
Continuous Blast	Distress signal

Figure 45: Sound Signals

VISUAL SIGNALS: FLAGS AND LIGHTS

Each nautical flag has both an alphanumeric value and a specific meaning. For example, the "C" flag is also used to mean "Yes." The meanings and value of each flag are found in the appendix. The chart also includes the phonetic pronunciation (used over the radio to avoid confusion) and Morse Code for each letter and number.

Flag communication can be one way, e.g. simply alerting other boats that there's a "diver below," or a more sophisticated two way dialog. The latter is rare, and there is no need for a recreational sailor to memorize the flag meanings, but the chart should be kept onboard for reference.

Lights communicate the type and size of the boat, as well as its position and heading. There are many different light configurations for specific types of commercial boats, but in general, larger (and therefore more dangerous) vessels have more lights than smaller ones. It's more important to be sure that you're displaying the proper lights than to memorize all the possible light configurations for other boats. For a complete list of all possible light configurations, see the USCG Navigation Rules found at:

http://www.uscg.mil/directives/cim/16000-16999/cim_16672_2d.pdf.

Boat lights are described based on their position on the boat and the field of view that they shine into, as illustrated in Figure 46. Notice how the side lights always conform to the stand on and give way zones. The masthead light can be an all around light, but frequently only covers 225° facing forward, particularly when it is coupled with a stern light.

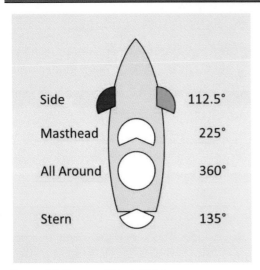

Figure 46: Types of Boat Lights

As mentioned earlier, lights should be – and are usually legally required to be – displayed from sunset to sunrise and during periods of restricted visibility, such as fog. The light configurations for sailboats are shown in the appendix. Most recreational boats will be covered by these few simple categories.

Position and heading are communicated by the light colors, as discussed in the section on stand on and give way zones. You can also judge the relative speed of a boat based on how its position changes with respect to your own.

Radio Communication

Working a radio is another topic that can easily fill an entire course on its own, but I'll just give a brief overview of the essentials here. Hopefully you'll never need to use your radio in an emergency, but like a good boy scout, you should be prepared in case you have to. And even if you

never face an emergency yourself, you may be able to help other boats in need of assistance. You might also need to get in touch with a marina or harbor operator at some point.

There are three types of messages that are permissible transmissions over the radio: *safety, operations*, and *commerce*. Radio channels, or more formally, different frequencies, are allocated for each type of use. Most radios can be controlled by selecting a channel (which is then automatically converted to a frequency) or by controlling the frequency directly.

A summary of the different radio channels and their usage is given in Figure 47. Always use the appropriate channel for all radio communications. Recreational sailors will never use commercial channels, although you're free to listen if you think there's pertinent information being broadcast (e.g., if there's a commercial vessel in your immediate vicinity). You may need to use operational channels to get permission to enter a harbor, get a mooring assignment when visiting a marina, etc.

That leaves safety communication, which is further broken down into three types of communications: *distress, urgency*, and *safety*. The keywords *Mayday, Pan Pan*, and *Security* (pronounced like the French word sécurité), indicate each type of safety communication, respectively.

NON-COMMERCIAL VHF-FM RADIO CHANNELS	
Type of Message	**Suitable Channels**
Distress, Urgency, Safety, and Calling	16
Alternate Calling Channel (Non Commercial Vessels)	9
Intership Safety	6
Coast Guard Liaison	22A
Non-Commercial[1]	68, 69, 71, 72, 78A
Public Correspondence (Marine Operator)	24, 25, 26, 27, 28, 84, 85, 86, 87, 88[2]
Port Operations	1, 5[3], 11, 12, 14, 20[4], 63, 65, 66, 73, 74, 77[5]
Navigational	13
Maritime Control	17
Digital Selective Calling	70
Weather[6]	WX-1, WX-2, WX-3
1. Working channels for recreational boats only. Other channels are reserved for working vessels.	
2. Only for use in the Great Lakes, the St. Lawrence Seaway, and Puget Sound and its approaches.	
3. Available only in the Houston and New Orleans areas.	
4. Channel 20 used only for ship-to-coast messages.	
5. Channel 77 is limited to intership communications to and from pilot boats.	
6. Weather channels are "receive only."	
Source: US Coast Guard	

Figure 47: Radio Channels

Figure 48 describes the type of situation when each safety call should be used, along with other procedure words used during radio communication. For example, Mayday calls should only be used when there is grave imminent danger and immediate help is needed, i.e. the boat is sinking or someone just had a heart attack. In most other issues, such as some MOB situations, you should use Pan Pan.

In the appendix, the formats of Mayday and Pan Pan calls are outlined. You'll notice the reference to a radio call sign, but if you haven't been given one by the FCC (which you probably haven't), just leave it out. These forms should be filled out and kept onboard in case of an emergency. Security calls are usually given only by the Coast Guard.

After you give a distress call, the responder will typically provide further instructions, such as moving to another radio channel to avoid clogging the emergency channel. If you ever hear a distress call, it is your obligation to respond. However, you should wait a few moments to allow for someone else who may be more capable of assisting to respond. Usually they will.

RADIO PROCEDURE WORDS	
Word	**Meaning**
Mayday	DISTRESS signal used when there is grave and immediate danger, requesting IMMEDIATE ASSISTANCE.
Pan Pan	URGENCY signal used when a ship or person is in JEOPARDY.
Security	SAFETY signal used for IMPORTANT navigation information weather warnings.
Out	This is the end of my transmission to you. No answer is required or expected.
Over	This is the end of my transmission and a response is expected. Go ahead, transmit. Omit when it is clearly not needed.
Roger	I received your last transmission ok.
Wilco	Your last message has been received, understood, and will be complied with.
This Is	This transmission is from the station whose name and call sign follows immediately.
Figures	Figures or numbers follow, for example, "Vessel length is FIGURES two three feet."
Speak Slower	Your transmission is difficult to understand. Speak slower.
Say Again	Repeat.
Words Twice	It is difficult to understand you. Give each phrase twice.
I Spell	I shall spell the next word phonetically. Used when a proper name is important in the message. "Moat name is Martha. I SPELL Mike, Alpha, Romeo, Tango, Hotel, Alpha."
Wait	I must pause for a few seconds. Stand by for further transmission.
Wait Out	I must pause for longer than a few seconds. I will call you back.
Affirmative	You are correct, or what you have transmitted is correct.
Negative	No.
	Source: US Coast Guard

Figure 48: Radio Procedure Words

OTHER DISTRESS SIGNALS

Aside from radio calls, there are other universal signals of distress that you can use (and should respond to). These are given in the appendix along with some that have already been mentioned.

NAVIGATION AND PILOTAGE

Getting from point A to point B without running into anything above or below the water. That's the essence of navigation. It's all about figuring out where you are, where you want to go, how to get there, and what obstacles to avoid.

AIDS TO NAVIGATION

Visual markings on the water and along the coast such as buoys and waterway mark are known as aids to navigation or **ATONs**. They come in all shapes and sizes and are most useful simply as unique position identifiers when trying to locate your location on a chart. Also of importance are regulatory markings indicating top speed and other restrictions in channels or marinas.

The appendix contains Coast Guard summary charts of the ATONs used in the US, including their corresponding chart markings. For a more complete explanation, see the Coast Guard reference at:

http://www.uscgboating.org/assets/1/workflow_staging/Publications/486.PDF

RED RIGHT RETURNING

It can be confusing deciphering the specific meaning of an ATON, but fortunately, the most important information – which side you should be on – is easy to figure out.

Markings that direct you to pass on one side or the other will be either red or green. They are used to prevent boats from running aground or hitting an underwater obstruction. Most ATONs you'll see will be red or green or will be marina markings regulating speed, wake, etc. To figure out which side of a colored marking you should pass on, there is a simple system called **Red Right Returning**.

Here's how it works. When returning from the open sea to a marina or channel (or going up stream when you're on a river), you keep red markings, on your right (i.e., starboard).

You may be thinking, "That's great, but what if I'm not returning?" Well the nice thing about Red Right Returning is that it works kind of like a math equality. If you change any one of the words, you then have to change another one (only one) to get it to "balance."

For example, if you are leaving instead of returning, you would then have to change either red to green or right to left. So you could have either Red Left Leaving, or Green Right Leaving. You can then make sure to either have a red marker on you right or a green marker on your left. Whether you're leaving or returning, or whether you see a red or green marker, you can use Red Right Returning to determine which side to pass on.

Just remember that the direction, right, means that you have to have the *marker on your right*, NOT that you should pass to the right side of the marker.

You can also use Red Right Returning to deduce information about the waterway you're on. Sometimes it's obvious which side of a marker you should pass on because there's a bank or other land formation on the opposite side. In that case, you can use Red Right Returning to determine what direction is considered "Returning" for the particular waterway you're on if there's any ambiguity.

If you happen to be color blind or for some reason the color of the marking is unclear, you can use

the numbers as an alternative. *Red markings should have even numbers*, and *green markings should have odd numbers*. Also note that the numbers on colored markings should be increase as you progress inland, which is considered the "Returning" direction.

NAVIGATION

Navigation – figuring out where you are and how to get where you want to go – has been greatly simplified with modern technology. GPS systems are widely available in both handheld portable units or as built in onboard instrumentation and require almost no nautical knowledge to use.

Most recreational sailors don't need to pinpoint exact location anyway, but if you ever do want to sail further into the unknown, it helps to have a basic understanding of traditional navigation or **charting**. I won't go into too much detail – there are many resources available for those who wish to become navigation experts – but I'll just explain the basic concepts.

Essentially, charting involves using visible landmarks to figure out a boat's location. It's all simple geometry, but does require some thorough bookkeeping. There are also other complications like correcting your boat's compass (a magnet) depending on where on Earth you're located.

Geometrically, you need only two reference points to identify the location of your boat (more points improve accuracy). After finding the angle between each point and the boat using a compass, you draw a line from each know reference point on a nautical chart (i.e., a map) and the intersection of those lines is your boat's location. You now have a **fix**, or an estimate of your boat's location at a specific time.

By keeping track of your speed, heading, and the amount of time that has passed since your last fix, you can estimate your path through the water. This process is known as **dead reckoning**.

You can easily estimate a course using a nautical chart and your boat speed in knots. As discussed earlier, a knot is simply a nautical mile – or one minute of latitude – per hour. The fact that nautical maps are marked in longitude and latitude makes this process very simple. Of course, a complicating factor is the difference between longitude and latitude. While surface distance between latitude lines constant everywhere on Earth, longitude lines converge at the poles. Precise charting takes this into account.

In summary, charting is a very simple idea – triangulating a position and extrapolating using speed and direction – but gets complicated when you take into account all the slight adjustments and that need to be made. You're much better off using the GPS if you can.

SAILING GLOSSARY

abeam:	The direction off the side (beam) of the boat.
aft:	Toward the stern of the boat.
ahead:	Forward, relative to the boat.
alee:	Away from the wind.
anchor bend:	A type of hitch knot. Also known as a round turn and two half hitches.
angle of attack:	The angle between the sail chord and the wind direction.
apparent wind:	The wind experienced by a moving object (the boat). Formally, the vector sum of the true wind and the boat speed.
astern:	Backwards, relative to the boat.
ATONs:	Aids to Navigation. Buoys, day marks, lighthouses, etc.
aweather:	Towards the wind.
backwinded:	A sail is backwinded when wind wills the wrong side of the sail.
ballast:	Weight on board a boat, typically used to provide lateral stability.
beam:	The side of a boat.
beam reach:	A point of sail directly perpendicular to the wind.
bear away:	Turning away from the wind.
beating:	The point of sail closest to the wind that a sailboat is capable of sailing.
belay:	To fix a line around a cleat.
berthing:	Guiding a boat into a slip.
bitt:	A ring on an anchor that an anchor line can be tied to.
blocks:	Pulleys.

boom: A horizontal bar connected to the mast that supports and controls the foot of the mainsail.

boom vang: A type of downhaul connected to the boom.

bow: The forwardmost point of a boat.

bowline: A type of knot that forms a ring at the end of a line.

bridle: A ring at the end of the spinnaker pole that's used to connect the topping lift and downhaul.

broad reach: The point of sail between a beam reach and running.

cabin: The hollowed out passenger area of the hull on larger boats.

catamaran: A twin-hulled boat.

cauterize: To seal the end of a line by melting the wax that is part of the strands making up the line.

centerboard: A adjustable fin, typically made of wood, that protrudes from the bottom of the hull.

charting: The process of navigation using nautical charts.

chord: An imaginary straight line connecting the leach and luff of a sail.

cleat: Hardware used to fix lines.

clew: The leeward corner at the foot of a sail.

clew outhaul: A line used to pull the mainsail clew to the end of the mast.

close hauled: See beating.

close reach: The point of sail between a beam reach and beating.

clove hitch: A type of hitch knot used to tie a line to a post.

cockpit: The area of a boat where the captain sits and operates the tiller or wheel.

come about: To tack.

cunningham:	A type of downhaul that is sometimes found in place of the boom vang.
daysail:	A sailing trip where you leave and return in the same day.
dead reckoning:	A method for estimating a boat's location by extrapolating from a previous fix using boat speed, heading, and time.
downhaul:	Rigging that pulls down on the boom or spinnaker pole.
downwind:	See leeward.
draft:	The depth of a sail's curvature.
driving force:	The component of wind force acting along a boat's heading.
ease off:	To let out the sheets, increasing the sheeting angle.
fall off:	See bear away.
figure eight:	A type of stopper knot shaped like the number eight.
fix:	During navigation, when you know your boat's location, you're said to have a fix.
foot:	The bottom edge of a sail
foredeck:	The forward area of a boat's deck ahead of the mast.
foresail:	Any sail that flies in ahead of the mast.
forward:	Towards the front of the boat.
fouled:	An anchor that is caught on the bottom of the see is fouled.
furling:	A furling sail can be coiled around one of its edges like a window curtain.
genoa:	A very large foresail.
give way:	To change direction in order to get out of the way of another boat.
gunwale:	The top edge of a boat's hull.
gybe:	The maneuver of turning a sailboat so that the stern passes through the wind.
halyard:	A line used to raise a sail.

harden up: To bring in a sheet, reducing the sheeting angle.

head up: Turning towards the wind, without tacking.

heading: The direction in which a boat is pointing.

heave to: A maneuver where the jib is backwinded and the boat is stalled in place to allow the captain to leave the helm safely.

heel: When the boat rotates sideways, tipping over, it is heeling.

heeling forces: Forces that tend to cause the boat to tip over.

hike out: Using a system of harnesses and lines to hang over the beam of a small sailboat in order to counteract heeling forces.

hull: The main floating structural component of a boat.

in irons: When a sailboat is pointed into the wind at too close an angle, it cannot generate and sail forces and is said to be in irons.

jib: A small to moderately sized foresail.

keel: A heavily weighted, fixed fin on the bottom of the hull that provides ballast on larger boats.

knots: Nautical miles per hour.

lead line: A line that is dropped to the seafloor in order to check the water depth and seafloor composition.

leech: The leeward edge of a sail.

leeward: Away from the wind.

leeway: The sideways drift of a boat resulting from sail side forces not entirely being offset by heel or centerboard forces.

lines: Ropes.

long blast: A sound signal lasting 4 to 6 seconds.

loosen up: See ease off.

luff: The windward edge of a sail.

luffing: A sail that is not catching any wind and is flapping like a flag is luffing.

mainsail: The primary sail connected to the mast and the boom.

mooring: A permanent anchor with a floating buoy that boats can hook up to.

nautical mile: The distance equal to one minute of lattitude, or 1.15 miles.

pendant: A short line connected to a mooring that boats can connect to without hitting the mooring.

pivot point: The point about which a boat or car rotates during turns.

point of sail: A boat's heading with respect to the wind direction.

port: The left side of a boat when viewed looking forward from the stern.

prop walk: The sideways force created by spinning propeller blades.

prop wash: The water jet created behind a propeller.

Red Right Returning: A rule of thumb for determining on which side of daymarkers to pass.

reefing: The process of reducing the area of the mainsail exposed to the wind by dropping it partially and tying the unsecured portion to the mast.

reefing knot: A knot that joins two lines of the same size, or two ends of the same line as during reefing.

rigging: Ropes, cables, pulleys, etc. used to hold up and control the sails.

righting forces: Forces that counteract heeling forces.

rudder: A moveable fin and the rear of the boat used as the primary method of controlling its direction.

rules of the road: The rules determining the stand on and give way vessels when boats' paths cross.

running: Sailing directly away from the wind.

running rigging: Any adjustable rigging used to raise or control the sails.

sheet bend: A type of knot used to connect two lines of different sizes.

sheet in: See harden up.

sheeting angle: The angle between the sail chord and the boat's centerline.

sheets: Lines used to control the sheeting angle.

short blast: A sound signal lasting 1 second or less.

shrouds: Side stays.

side force: The component of wind force acting perpendicular to a boat's heading.

slip: An area between two docks where a boat is parked.

spinnaker: A large foresail that replaces the jib or genoa and acts like a parachute, only functioning on downwind tacks.

spinnaker pole: A pole that holds the spinnaker clew away from the mast.

spreaders: Vertical bars near the top of the mast that separate side stays.

square knot: See reefing knot.

stand on: To continue on a heading without adjusting course.

standing rigging: Rigging used to hold up the mast.

starboard: The right side of a boat when viewed looking forward from the stern.

stays: Cables connected to the mast to hold in in place.

stern: The rear end of a boat.

storm jib: A very small jib used during a storm that catches minimal wind but improves control over sailing with the mainsail alone.

streamers: See telltales.

tack: 1) The windward corner at the foot of a sail.

                          2) A boat's heading with respect to the wind.

3) The maneuver of turning a sailboat so that the bow passes through the wind.

telltales: Very light lines used to read the local behavior of the wind in their immediate vicinity.

tiller: A long rod attached to the top of the rudder used to control it.

toot: See short blast.

topping lift: Rigging that pulls up on the boom or spinnaker pole.

topside: When a boat is heeled over, the side of the boat that is further out of the water. The windward side of the boat.

trapezing: See hiking out

trim: 1) The shape and sheeting angle of a sail.

2) To adjust the shape or sheeting angle of a sail.

trimaran: A three-hulled boat.

true wind: The wind that would be experienced by a stationary object.

tufts: See telltales.

twist: The degree to which a sail is curved along the vertical direction.

upwind: See windward.

whisker pole: A pole that holds the clew of a large jib or genoa away from the mast.

winches: Racheting spools used to bring in lines that can't be pulled in by hand.

windward: Towards the wind.

wing-and-wing: See running.

wools: See telltales.

yarns: See telltales.

APPENDIX

COILING AND STORING A LINE

COILING AND HANGING A LINE

FIGURE EIGHT KNOT

BELAYING A CLEAT

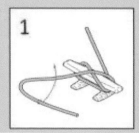 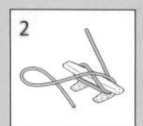 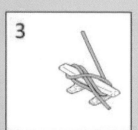

CLOVE HITCH

REEFING (SQUARE) KNOT

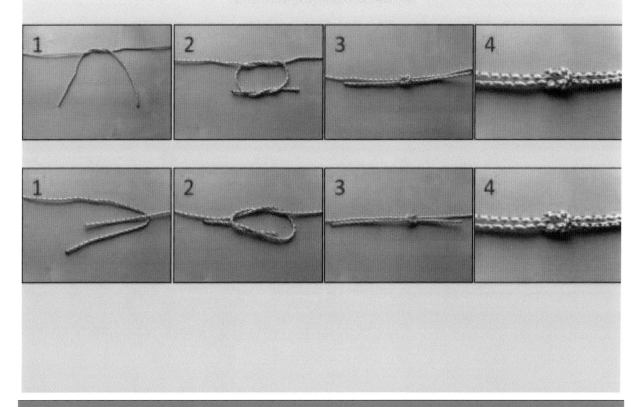

SHEET BEND

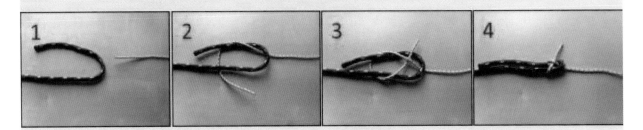

BOWLINE KNOT

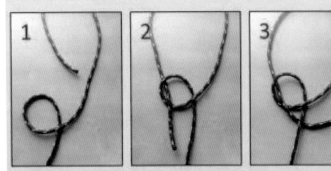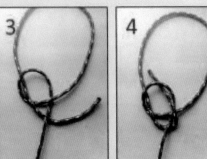

ANCHOR BEND

AL FAH

I have a diver down; keep clear and pass at low speed

BRAH VOH

I am loading, unloading, or carrying dangerous goods

CHAR LEE

Yes; confirmation of preceding signal

DELL TAH

Keep clear, I am maneuvering with difficulty

ECK OH

I am altering course to starboard

FOKS TROT

I am disabled, communicate with me

GOLF

I require a pilot or (on a fishing vessel) I am hauling nets

HO TELL

I have a pilot on board

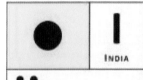

IN DEE AH

I am altering course to port

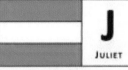

JEW LEE ETT

I am on fire and have dangerous cargo on board; keep clear

KEY LOH

I wish to communicate with you

LEE MAH

You should stop your vessel immediately

MIKE

My vessel is stropped and making no way through the water

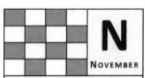

NO VEM BER

No; the preceding signal should be read in the negative

OSS CAH

Man overboard

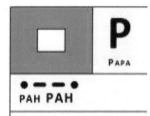

PAH PAH

I am about to put to sea

KEH BECK

My vessel is healthy and I request clearance to come ashore

ROW ME OH

No allocated meaning

SEE AIR RAH

I am going astern under power

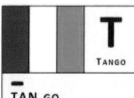

TAN GO

Keep clear, I am engaged in pair trawling

U UNIFORM

● ● —

YOU NEE FORM

You are running into danger

V VICTOR

● ● ● —

VIK TAH

I require assistance

W WHISKEY

● — —

WISS KEY

I require medical assistance

X XRAY

— ● ● —

ECKS RAY

Stop carrying out your intentions and watch for my signals

Y YANKEE

— ● — —

YANG KEY

I am dragging my anchor

Z ZULU

— — ● ●

ZOO LOO

I require a tug or (on a fishing vessel) I am shooting nets

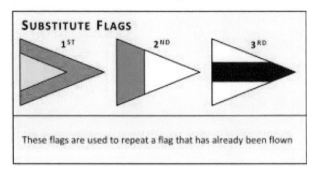

SUBSTITUTE FLAGS

1ST   2ND   3RD

These flags are used to repeat a flag that has already been flown

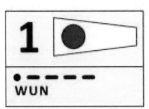

1

● — — — —

WUN

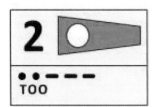

2

● ● — — —

TOO

3

● ● ● — —

THUH REE

4

● ● ● ● —

FO WER

5

● ● ● ● ●

FI YIV

6

— ● ● ● ●

SIX

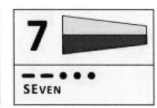

7

— — ● ● ●

SEVEN

8

— — — ● ●

ATE

9

— — — — ●

NINER

0

— — — — —

ZERO

Boat Type	Light Description	Illustration
Under 7 meters (~23 feet) without built in lights	Handheld	
Sailing vessel under 20 meters (65 1/2 feet)	Side and stern lights (all around colored masthead lights optional) OR tricolor masthead light	
Sailboat Under Power	Side and stern lights plus masthead light	
Sailboat Under Power (less than 12 meters, ~39 feet)	Side lights and all around masthead light	

Distress Communication (Mayday) Form

Speak: Slowly – Clearly – Calmly

1. Make certain your radio is turned on.
2. Select **VHF-FM Channel 16** or **2182 kHz for your SSB**.
3. Press microphone button and say: **MAYDAY – MAYDAY – MAYDAY**
4. Say: **THIS IS** _____ _____ _____

    (Your boat name, spoken three times.)

    _____

    (Your call sign, spoken once)

5. Say: **MAYDAY** _____

    (Your boat name, spoken once).

6. **TELL WHERE YOU ARE.** (What navigational aids or landmarks are you near? What direction and distance are you from a landmark" What is your latitude and longitude? What are your Loran coordinates?)
7. **STATE THE NATURE OF YOUR DISTRESS.** (e.g., taking on water, siking, fire, etc.)
8. **GIVE NUMBER OF PEOPLE ONBOARD AND CONDITIONS OF ANY INJURED.**
9. **ESTIMATE CURRENT SEAWORTHINESS OF YOUR BOAT.**
10. **BRIEFLY DESCRIBE YOUR BOAT:**

    _____ **FEET;**

    (Length)

    _____ _____ **HULL;**

    (Type)   (Color)

    _____ **TRIM;**

    (Color)

    _____ **MASTS;**

    (Number)

    _____

    (Anything else you think will help rescuers find you.)

11. Say: **I WILL BE LISTENING ON CHANNEL 16.**
12. End message by saying: **THIS IS** _____ **OVER.**

    (Your boat name and call sign)

13. Release microphone button and listen. Someone should answer. **IF THEY DO NOT, REPEAT CALL, BEGINNING AT ITEM #1 ABOVE. IF THERE IS STILL NO ANSWER, CHECK TO SEE IF YOUR SET IS TURNED ON, IS ON HIGH POWER, AND IS ON CHANNEL 16 IF IS VHF-FM OR 2182 kHz IF IT IS SSB.**

Urgency Communication (Pan-Pan) Form

Speak: Slowly – Clearly – Calmly

1. Make certain your radio is turned on.
2. Select **VHF-FM Channel 16** or **2182 kHz for your SSB.**
3. Press microphone button and say: **PAN-PAN – PAN-PAN – PAN-PAN**
4. Say: **TO ALL STATIONS** (or a particular station)
5. Say: **THIS IS** _____ _____ _____

   (Your boat name, spoken three times.)

   _____

   (Your call sign, spoken once)
6. **STATE THE URGENCY MESSAGE** (describe your problem)
7. **TELL WHERE YOU ARE.** (What navigational aids or landmarks are you near? What direction and distance are you from a landmark" What is your latitude and longitude? What are your Loran coordinates?)
8. **BRIEFLY DESCRIBE YOUR BOAT:**

   _____ **FEET;**

   (Length)

   _____ _____ **HULL;**

   (Type)   (Color)

   _____ **TRIM;**

   (Color)

   _____ **MASTS;**

   (Number)

   _____

   (Anything else you think will help rescuers find you.)
9. End message by saying: **THIS IS** _____ **OVER.**

   (Your boat name and call sign)
10. Release microphone button and listen. Someone should answer. **IF THEY DO NOT, REPEAT CALL, BEGINNING AT ITEM #1 ABOVE. IF THERE IS STILL NO ANSWER, CHECK TO SEE IF YOUR SET IS TURNED ON, IS ON HIGH POWER, AND IS ON CHANNEL 16 IF IS VHF-FM OR 2182 kHz IF IT IS SSB.**

RED STAR
SHELLS

FOG HORN
CONTINUOUS
SOUNDING

FLAMES ON
A VESSEL

GUN
FIRED AT
INTERVALS OF
1 MIN.

ORANGE
BACKGROUND
BLACK BALL
AND SQUARE

SOS

SOS

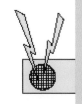

"MAYDAY"
BY RADIO

PARACHUTE
RED FLARE

DYE
MARKER
(ANY COLOR)

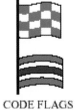

CODE FLAGS
NOVEMBER
CHARLIE

SQUARE FLAG
AND BALL

WAVE
ARMS

RADIO-
TELEGRAPH
ALARM

RADIO-
TELEPHONE
ALARM

POSITION
INDICATING
RADIO
BEACON

SMOKE

U.S. AIDS TO NAVIGATION SYSTEM
on navigable waters except Western Rivers

LATERAL SYSTEM AS SEEN ENTERING FROM SEAWARD

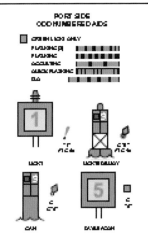

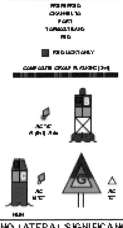

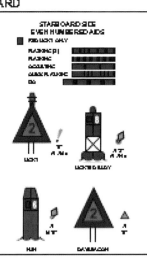

AIDS TO NAVIGATION HAVING NO LATERAL SIGNIFICANCE

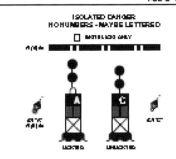

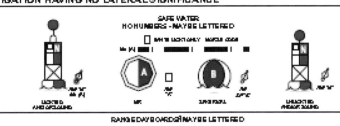

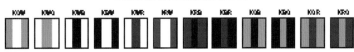

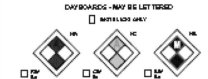

Aids to Navigation marking the Intracoastal Waterway (ICW) display unique yellow symbols to distinguish them from aids marking other waters. Yellow triangles △ indicate aids should be passed by keeping them on the starboard (right) hand of the vessel. Yellow squares □ indicate aids should be passed by keeping them on the port (left) hand of the vessel. A yellow horizontal band ▭ provides no lateral information, but simply identifies aids as marking the ICW.

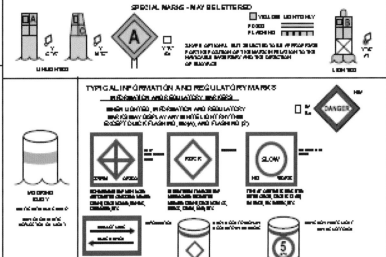

U.S. AIDS TO NAVIGATION SYSTEM
on the Western River System

AS SEEN ENTERING FROM SEAWARD

PORT SIDE
OR RIGHT DESCENDING BANK

LIGHT — LIGHTED BUOY — CAN

176.9
MILE BOARD

PREFERRED CHANNEL
JUNCTIONS AND OBSTRUCTIONS
COMPOSITE GROUP FLASHING (2+1)

PREFERRED CHANNEL TO STARBOARD TOPMOST BAND GREEN	PREFERRED CHANNEL TO PORT TOPMOST BAND RED

DAYBOARDS HAVING NO LATERAL SIGNIFICANCE

STARBOARD SIDE
OR LEFT DESCENDING BANK

LIGHT — LIGHTED BUOY — NUN

123.5
MILE BOARD

SPECIAL MARKS–MAYS LETTERED

MOORING BUOY

TYPICAL INFORMATION AND REGULATORY MARKS
INFORMATION AND REGULATORY MARKERS

BOAT EXCLUSION AREA

DANGER

CONTROLLED AREA

INFORMATION

STATE WATERS

Printed in Great Britain
by Amazon

27979404R00055